INTERNAL MIGRATION
AND
ECONOMIC DEVELOPMENT

A Theoretical and Empirical Study

Dominick Salvatore

Fordham University

Published in the U.S.A.
by the University Press of America
Washington, D.C.

ISBN (Perfect): 0-8191-1641-6
ISBN (Cloth): 0-8191-1640-8
LCN: 81-40066

Printed in the United States of America

CONTENTS

PREFACE

The aim of this study is to examine the relative importance of the various socio-economic determinants of the large post-war labor migration from the South to the North of Italy and analyze the effects of such migration on the past and prospective development of the South and on the size of regional differences.

The effect of internal migration on the development of the South and on North-South differences has been the subject of great (and often emotional) controversy. On the one hand, there are those who assert that labor migration from the South to the North and to other nations has drained the South of much of its development potential and has hindered its past and future development prospects. On the other, there are those who feel that migration has relieved the South of some of its surplus labor and brightened its development prospects. This controversy has been as much the result of incomplete or faulty theoretical analysis as it is of the lack of rigorous empirical testing. In general, labor migration can harm or enhance the development prospects of the area of emigration and can increase or reduce regional differences, depending on the circumstances under which it takes place.

Chapter I presents, evaluates and seeks to resolve the theoretical controversy on the causes and effects of internal labor migration in general. Chapter II introduces and evaluates various types and variables of models of internal migration. Chapter III develops a simultaneous-equations model of internal labor migration in Italy. In Chapter IV, the model is estimated and validated and used to analyze the effect of migration on the development of the South and on North-South differences. Chapter V examines the effectiveness of various policies to stimulate the development of the South and to reduce North-South differences. The more technical econometric aspects of the study are put in the appendices, so that the reader with little or no knowledge of econometrics can profitably go through the text.

Though the study deals with Italy, its results and conclusions are of general relevance since Italy is often considered a prototype of dualistic development. This study is also the first simultaneous-equations model applied to time series data. Furthermore, the simultaneity nature of the model allows for the objective evaluation of the effects as well as the causes of internal labor migration. This is recognized as one of the most important, difficult and understudied research areas in internal migration, the world over.

This study represents, in a way, the natural conclusion of the author's work on internal migration in general, and internal migration in Italy, in particular. His interest started with a Senior Fulbright Research Award to Italy for the 1975–6 academic year (on leave from Fordham University in New York) and included six articles in leading American and European economic journals, two presentations at the annual meetings of the American Econometric

Society (Atlantic City in 1976, Chicago in 1978) and lectures at various universities in Italy, the United States and Yugoslavia.

The author is grateful to the Commission for Educational and Cultural Exchange between Italy and the United States for the Senior Fulbright Research Award to Italy. Professor V. Siesto, M. Brancoli, and Dr. G. Marrocchi provided invaluable help through the years. I had many stimulating conversations on the topic of internal migration with Professor A. Golini and Professor C. Pace of the University of Rome, Professor G. Colombo of the University of Bari, and Professor A. Falciglia of the University of Venice. Dr. G. Busso and Dr. G. DeSouza have also provided help at various stages of the work. One of the most exhilarating experiences of doing research in Italy is being exposed (subject to contagion) to the radiance and warmth of its people. Giorgio Provenziani is but one such a person.

I. INTERNAL MIGRATION
IN REGIONAL AND
NATIONAL DEVELOPMENT

1. Theoretical considerations

In most nations of the world, including the most advanced, there usually exist some regional differences in the level of development and standard of living. This is as true for the United States, West Germany, France and England as it is for Italy, Spain, Brazil and India. These regional differences are generally not very great in the most advanced nations and have been declining.[1] For example, in the United States, the differences in living standards between the North and the South are now below 10 percent and are well on the way to being completely eliminated.

In some nations, on the other hand, regional differences are very large and persistent and show no sign of being quickly reduced or eliminated. Classic examples of such dualistic development are Italy and Brazil. Real per capita incomes as well as most other socio-economic indexes of economic development are between 60 and 80 percent of the national average in the Italian South and the Brazilian Northeast, and show little sign of abatement.

These regional differences usually give rise to interregional flows of labor and capital which affect both the rate of regional and national growth and development. It is at this point that a great deal of controversy arises.

(a) Neoclassical theory

According to neoclassical economic theory,[2] interregional flows of labor and capital should benefit the more developed as well as the less developed region, and thus the nation as a whole. The reasoning is as follows. Suppose we had two regions that were completely isolated (no interregional factor mobility or trade), that we had only two homogeneous factors (L and K) and that one

---

[1] Jeffrey Williamson, "Regional Inequality and the Process of National Development," *Economic Development and Cultural Change," XIII* (1965), pp. 3-83.

[1] See Dominick Salvatore, *Microeconomic Theory* (New York: McGraw-Hill, 1974); Second Edition, 1982. Dominick Salvatore, *International Economics* (New York: McGraw-Hill, 1975); and Dominick Salvatore and Edward Dowling, *Development Economics* (New York: McGraw-Hill, 1977).

region had a much higher L/K ratio than the other; then the first region would have a lower marginal productivity of labor and therefore lower wages, and a higher marginal productivity of capital and therefore higher returns on capital than the second region (assuming that the same technology was used in both regions). If we now allowed for perfect mobility of factors, labor would flow out, and capital would flow in region one. As a result of these resource flows, the supply of L would fall (shift up) and the demand (or productivity of L) would increase (shift up) in region one. These would cause the return to labor to rise and the return to capital to fall in region one. In region two the exact opposite would take place. This would continue until the return to the homogeneous factor labor and capital would be exactly the same in region one and in region two. The result is that the more developed region is assured of an adequate supply of labor as well as an outlet for some of its capital to be invested in the less developed (and capital-poorer) region where returns on capital might be higher.

According to this neoclassical theory, the poorer region also benefits by being relieved of its surplus labor and from receiving capital inflows. These cause its real wages, incomes and standard of living to rise. Additional benefits to the less developed region result from emigrants' remittances and by the skills acquired by returning migrants.

(b) Myrdal's and Hirschman's theory

The opposite point of view from neoclassical theory is held by Myrdal, Hirschman and others. According to them, the net effect of the operation of the market mechanism is detrimental to the development of an underdeveloped region in an otherwise developed country.[3] In Myrdal's words:

> It is easy to see how expansion in one locality has 'backwash effects' in other localities. More specifically the movement of labor, capital, goods and services do not by themselves counteract the natural tendency to regional inequality. By themselves, migration, capital movements and trade *are rather the media through which the cumulative process evolves*—upward in the lucky regions and downward in the unlucky ones. In general if they have positive results for the former, their effect on the latter are negative.[4]

With regard to emigration Hirschman states:

> ... Northern progress may denude the South (the poor region) of its key technicians and managers as well as the more enterprising young men .... It becomes almost a certainty that the South will lose to the North first and foremost its more highly qualified people.[5]

[3] Gunnar Myrdal, *Rich Lands and Poor* (New York: Harper & Row, 1957), chapter III, and Albert O, Hirschman, *The Strategy of Economic Development* (New Haven: Yale University Press, 1958), chapter X.

[4] Gunnar Myrdal, *Rich Lands and Poor*, p. 27. The italics are mine.

[5] Albert O. Hirschman, *The Strategy of Economic Development*, pp. 188–89. The words in parenthesis are mine.

The movement of capital also has a deleterious effect on the less developed region:

> Capital movements tend to have a similar effect of increasing inequality. In the centers of expansion increased demand will spur investment.... In the other regions...the banking system, if not regulated to act differently, tends to become an instrument for siphoning off the savings from the poorer regions to the richer and more progressive ones where returns on capital are high and secure.[6]

Opposing these harmful, Backwash or Polarization Effects, there might be some beneficial, Spread or Trickling-Down Effects on the poorer region emanating from the more dynamic area:

> The favorable effects consist of the trickling-down of Northern progress: by far the most important of these effects is the increase of Northern purchases and investments in the South.... In addition, the North may absorb some of the disguised unemployed of the South and thereby raise the marginal productivity of labor and per capita consumption levels in the South.[7]

However, both Myrdal and Hirschman believe that the overall effect of the interregional movement of labor and capital is deleterious to the development of the poorer and less dynamic region, *under the normal conditions prevailing in these nations today* (i.e., low supply elasticities in agriculture, overpopulation, etc.)[8]

Indeed, the belief that interregional migration of labor (and capital) is detrimental to the development prospect of the poorer region is a widely accepted belief.[9]

In concluding his argument, Myrdal does postulate that the more developed a nation, the stronger the Spread Effects in its poorer region.[10] Despite this, the Backwash Effects on the poorer region normally exceed the Spread Effects even in a developed nation. The reasons why regional inequalities have tended to diminish in the more developed nations were (and are) because the interferences with the market mechanism (aid to the poorer

[6] Gunnar Myrdal, *Rich Lands and Poor*, pp. 27–28.

[7] Albert O. Hirschman, *The Strategy of Economic Development*, pp. 187–88.

[8] Gunnar Myrdal, *Rich Lands and Poor*, p. 26; and Albert O. Hirschman, *The Strategy of Economic Development*, pp. 188–90.

[9] United Nations, Economic Commission for Europe, *Economic Survey of Europe*, 1953 and 1954, pp. 130–37 and 152–53, respectively; Jose R. Lasuén, "Regional Income Inequality and the Problem of Growth in Spain," *Regional Science Association Papers and Proceedings*, 1961, pp. 177–80; Werner Baer, "Regional Inequality and Economic Growth in Brazil," *Economic Development and Cultural Change*, XII (1964), pp. 269 and 284; Jeffrey G. Williamson, "Regional Inequality and the Process of National Development," pp. 6–7; John Friedman, "A Generalized Theory of Polarized Development," *Growth Centers in Regional Economic Development* (New York: Free Press, 1972), p. 94.

[10] This is confirmed empirically by J. Williamson in "Regional Inequality and the Process of National Development," Part II.

regions) extended by the central government had to move against much weaker opposite forces (excess of Backwash over Spread Effects) in developed countries than in less developed countries; in addition, the aid that the central government of developed countries could provide to its underdeveloped regions was proportionately much larger than in the case of less developed countries.[11]

2. Evaluation

It is evident from what has been said that neoclassical economic theory and the position held by Myrdal and Hirschman represent diametrically opposing views as to the effect of interregional migration of labor (and capital) on regional and national development. According to neoclassical theory, such interregional flows are beneficial to the more developed as well as to the less developed region, and thus to the nation as a whole. According to Myrdal and Hirschman, interregional labor (and capital) migration increases the growth of the more developed region but harms the poorer region and generally retards the long-run development prospect of the nation as a whole. Both positions have a number of serious shortcomings and it may be impossible to determine on theoretical grounds alone, which of these views (if any) is *generally* valid.

(a) Evaluation of neoclassical analysis

Neoclassical analysis is based on several implicit assumptions. Some of the more important are: (1) the existence of identical technology in both regions, (2) perfect mobility of labor, capital and goods, and (3) homogeneous factors of production. Needless to say, these conditions usually do not hold completely and sometimes not even approximately in the real world. For example, the most advanced technology may not be available or utilized in the less developed region, capital may not flow from the richer region if labor is not as productive in the less developed region or if the less developed region faces political instability and terrorism. The validity of the neoclassical conclusions may then depend on how divergent a particular real world situation is from those theoretically implied. Since conditions vary from case to case, no general *a-priori* conclusions may be reached on theoretical grounds alone. Even if the neoclassical conclusions held in a particular case (and both regions benefitted from interregional labor and capital migration), regional inequalities may rise, fall or remain unchanged, depending on the relative rate of growth in each region. However, widening regional inequalities may be unacceptable today on political grounds, and the national government may still feel compelled and justified to intervene with special programs for the less developed region.

(b) Evaluation of Myrdal's and Hirschman's theory

Myrdal's and Hirschman's theory faces even more serious shortcomings than

---

[11] Gunnar Myrdal, *Rich Lands and Poor,* pp. 34–49.

neoclassical theory. According to Myrdal, the emigration of all workers, whether employed or unemployed, skilled or unskilled, is detrimental to the development of the poor region because emigrants embody human capital and their emigration adversely affects the age structure of the population of the area of emigration.[12] Such broad generalizations are incorrect. We could regard labor migration as harmful to the less developed region only if this labor could and would be productively employed in the region, and if its departure results in a reduction in the present and potential real per capital income of the poor region and adversely affects the structure of its economy. On the other hand, the emigration (out of the underdeveloped region and to the developed one) of dependents, unemployed workers (whether unskilled or skilled and when there are no short-run prospects of fruitfully employing them in the poor region), or surplus farm labor (with marginal product equal to zero)—this emigration will not reduce the total output of the less developed region. Since that total output will now be subdivided among the fewer people remaining, it will leave a higher average product or real income per capita in the poor region and should thus be regarded as beneficial to it. Even if we were dealing with *employed, unskilled or skilled workers,* as long as the number of unemployed workers *with comparable skills* still remaining in the backward region greatly exceed the number of those who emigrate, and as long as they are widely distributed over that region or are willing to move to those areas of the poor region where job opportunities open up—as long as these conditions are met, then unemployed workers with similar skills can replace the employed workers who emigrate and the total output of the poor region would not or should not fall. Again, since the unchanged output is now subdivided among the fewer people remaining in the poor region, it will increase the average real per capita income of this area and this will also be regarded as beneficial to the poor region.

It is true that these migrant workers embody a great deal of human capital and that the poor region bears the cost of raising, educating and training these workers. However, without emigration, the less developed region would face the additional burden of sustaining these unemployed or underemployed workers. In the long run, of course, it would be much more advantageous if the growth in the labor force would coincide more closely with the growth of employment opportunities in the less developed region.

What would be harmful to the less developed region is the emigration of skilled workers and professional people, who were either employed at the time of their emigration (or for whom profitable employment would soon have been found), and who were earning (or could soon have been expected to have earned) an income higher than the average income in the underdeveloped region. This emigration would be harmful to the poor region because it would cause a fall (or prevent as high a rise as otherwise possible) in the average real per capita income of the people remaining in the backward region and would

[12] Gunnar Myrdal, *Rich Lands and Poor,* pp. 27–28; and Gunnar Myrdal, *An International Economy* (New York: Harper & Row, 1956), pp. 94–95.

also adversely affect the overall skill composition of its economy.[13] An additional harmful effect on the poor region would result if the best trained, most intelligent and hardworking workers within each job category would leave.

(c) The interregional flow of capital and migration

Even the emigration of unemployed and underemployed labor could be harmful to the less developed region if such migration were accompanied by capital outflows from the poorer region. It can be argued that such capital could be utilized to generate more jobs, eliminating or reducing the need for such labor migration. Thus, it is impossible to determine whether or not labor migration is harmful to the development of the poor region without also knowing whether this is accompanied by capital outflows. However, even here, there is a great deal of disagreement. As seen earlier, neoclassical theory postulates a capital inflow to the less developed region while Myrdal and Hirschman predict an outflow. This disagreement might be resolved by distinguishing three different situations.

Case 1. Capital, which could productively be utilized in the less developed region, flows instead to the more developed region because of higher and more secure returns. This capital outflow is harmful to the poor region and exemplifies Myrdal's and Hirschman's position.

Case 2. The marginal productivity and demand for capital is lower in the less developed than in the more developed region, but the supply of capital is so much lower in the less developed region that the return on capital is higher in the less developed region. This may lead to a capital inflow into the poorer region which would either increase the K/L ratio of employed labor or absorb more labor into the modern sector. This would benefit the poor region and confirm the neoclassical conclusion.

Case 3. If the structure of borrowing rates set by the monetary authorities[14] were higher than that which clears the market,[15] a surplus of investment funds over uses might arise in both the poorer and richer region and so no interregional movement of funds need occur. In this case, capital is not a "critical" shortage to foster development neither in the less nor in the more developed region.[16]

[13] For a more detailed and rigorous evaluation and extension of Myrdal's and Hirschman's theory, see Dominick Salvatore, "The Operation of the Market Mechanism and Regional Inequality," *Kyklos,* XXV (1972), pp. 518–36; and Dominick Salvatore, "Regional Inequality and the Market Mechanism," *Kyklos,* XXVI (1973), pp. 527–33.

[14] In the course of Open Market Operation, monetary authorities deal mostly in Treasury Bills, but all the other rates of interest are rather closely related and influenced by the rate on Treasury Bills.

[15] This might be so in order to curb inflationary pressures in the economy.

[16] For a more detailed discussion of these three cases and an evaluation of the effect of interregional capital movements on regional development, see Dominick Salvatore, "Interregional Capital Flows and Development," *Economia Internazionale,* XXIX (1976), pp. 66–80.

(d) Applicability of Myrdal's and Hirshman's theory

As can be gathered from what has been said, no amount of theoretical speculation can give us a generalized answer to these questions. That is, theoretical speculation alone could not tell us whether the interregional labor and capital flows *allows or causes* regional inequalities to *increase or decrease.* This depends on the underlying conditions prevailing in each particular nation affected by dualism. Since these conditions differ, the conclusion reached may differ from case to case. In short, what we need are empirical studies. However, Myrdal and Hirschman did not give any indication whatsoever as to the steps or techniques to follow in order to apply the theory to concrete cases. And a theory which has no empirically measureable content is not a very useful theory. Conclusive evidence that this is in fact the case can be gathered by turning to the area of application of this theory. There have been only one or two attempted (and not very successful) applications of this theory since it was expounded over twenty-five years ago.[17] This has been so not because the problem to which the theory refers is not an important problem whether we viewed it regionally or internationally (in fact a great deal of controversy has been and is raging, particularly between developed and underdeveloped countries with regard to this precise aspect of traditional economic theory[18]). Rather, the reason for this, I believe, is to be found exclusively in the fact that the authors of the theory did not give any indication as to how to apply it and because of the widespread lack of regional data.

The scarcity of empirical applications of this theory is to be contrasted with the incredible number of times that this theory is used 'en passant' to explain widening regional and international inequalities. It is considered as being self evident that if regional inequality in certain not very developed nations has increased over time this must have been (at least in part) *caused* by the fact that the operation of the market mechanism drains the poor region of its developmental resources.

In order for the theory of the Backwash and Spread Effects to be applicable to the real world a great deal of corrections and elaborations must be made on it. The corrections that are needed are implicit in the criticisms made above. The elaborations involve the breaking up of the aggregate movements (of people, capital, and commodities) discussed by Myrdal and Hirschman into their component parts; in precisely indicating how to actually measure these various submovements, and finally in specifying what data is needed to accomplish this.[19]

---

[17] Werner Baer, "Regional Inequality and Economic Growth in Brazil," *Economic Development and Cultural Change,* pp. 268–85.

[18] Harry G. Johnson, *Economic Policies toward Less Developed Countries* (New York: Frederick A. Praeger, Inc., 1967), especially chapters I-III.

[19] This elaboration and extension is beyond the scope of this volume and is carried out in Dominick Salvatore, "The Operation of the Market Mechanism and Regional Inequality."

3. Internal migration and the development of the South

(a) South-North labor migration

After more than 30 years of large-scale labor migration from the Italian South or Mezzogiorno (over 20 percent of its present labor force) the South-North unemployment and earnings differentials have remained virtually unchanged.[20] Even the large government effort (over 8 billion lire at current prices since 1950) only prevented the gap from growing larger.[21] The question of whether labor migration hindered the development of the South is extremely difficult to prove in view of the important qualitative component of the argument. Some of the quantitative aspects can be examined with the aid of Table 1. This shows that in 1951, and before the large-scale migration from the South started, the labor participation rates and the proportion of university and college degree holders in the South was lower than in the North. This was probably due to sociological reasons and to the relative lack of employment opportunities in the South. By 1971, the South had improved its position relative to the North. Thus, migration could only possibly have prevented a greater relative improvement in the South.

To the question of whether migration created an actual or potential shortage of labor in general and professional people and skilled labor in particular in the South, the tentative answer must be negative. It is easy enough to show this for unskilled labor. If we add to the number of openly unemployed in South one-fifth of the marginally employed (defined as those working 32 hours per week or less during the entire year) and subtract from this figure 2.5 percent of the labor force for frictional unemployment (certainly an overestimate), the resulting figure exceeds the number of emigrating workers by a multiple of at least 3 in each year and in each region of the South. Thus, an unemployed unskilled worker can easily take the place of an emigrating employed unskilled worker with little frictional loss to the South. Nor is this labor migration likely to create a potential labor shortage in the South in the near future. The South, with about 35 percent of the population of Italy, contributes about 60 percent of its natural population growth and the birthrate is falling only very slowly in the South.[22]

More crucial and difficult is to prove that migration from the South did not create an actual or potential shortage of professional people and skilled

[20] This, however, does not mean that migration had no effect since in its absence the gap might have been much different.

[21] This effort under the direction of the "Cassa per il Mezzogiorno" (Fund for the South) stressed first agriculture and infrastructures up to 1957, then special incentives to private investments in the South and finally direct investments. However, most of these direct investments were very capital-intensive (steel mills, petrochemicals, shipbuilding and other heavy industries in so-called industrial areas and nuclei) and, as it will be seen later, created relatively few industrial jobs in the South.

[22] Franco Pilloton, "Tendenze Evolutive del Mercato del Lavoro in Italia: 1951, 1971, 1991" in *Studi in Onore di Pasquale Saraceno* (Milano: Giuffre, 1975), pp. 755–89.

Table 1 North-South Comparison of Participation Rates and University and College Degree Holders per Thousand of the Population: 1951, 1961, 1971.

| | Labor Force Participation Rates | | | |
	1951	1961	1971	% Decline from 1951 to 1971
North	.489	.454	.389	22.78
South	.411	.380	.330	21.86
South as a % of North	84	84	85	—

| | University Degree Holders per Thousand of the Population | | | |
	1951	1961	1971	% Increase from 1951 to 1971
North	9.85	12.96	17.22	54.45
South	7.67	10.12	14.61	62.30
South as a % of North	78	78	85	—

| | College Degree Holders per Thousand of the Population | | | |
	1951	1961	1971	% Increase from 1951 to 1971
North	32.97	42.61	65.06	65.47
South	22.07	30.86	56.67	87.88
South as a % of North	67	72	87	—

Source: Population Census of 1951, 1961, 1971. (College degree holders include the graduates of technical institutes which supply most of the skilled workers.)

workers in the South. Professional people are here defined as those with a university degree. In 1958, the South had 32 percent of the labor force of Italy and 34 percent of the university degrees, of which 58 percent were in law and liberal arts. By 1974, the corresponding figures were 31, 36, and 62 percent respectively. Obviously, the South could not possibly absorb all of its law and liberal arts university-degree holders and some migration was therefore necessary. A "backwash effect" on the South could result if holders of technical degrees (engineers, doctors, etc.), that might be needed in the South also migrated. This possibility seems to be dispelled by an excellent stratified survey conducted in 1969 of 1,520 (15 percent) of the graduates from Southern universities in the year 1966.[23] This study found (among other things) that by 1969, the rate of open unemployment for the 1966 graduating class was 2.1 percent among engineers and architects, 2.7 percent for holders of other scientific degrees (excluding medicine), 5.2 percent for medicine and 5.4 percent for business administration. And this, 2.5 years after graduation, in years of economic boom, in the face of some emigration to the North (and other nations) and without considering the additional graduates of 1967, 1968 and 1969. In addition, of the emigrants who obtained a university degree in the South, 80 percent answered that they would return to the South if they were offered in the South a job similar to their present position in the North. Thus, it can be tentatively concluded that no shortage of professional people resulted or is likely to result in the near future in the South because of emigration.

Skilled workers are generated in the South by secondary schools including technical institutes and from on-the-job training. On-the-job training sufficient to create skilled workers of the type needed in modern economies are given in the South almost exclusively by the large-scale state-owned industries (chemical, steel, shipbuilding and mechanical). The real wages, the other benefits and the possibility of advancement in these industries are as good as in the North. These industries are also invariably located near large cities. Furthermore, these industries never complained of loss of their trained workers through emigration even though they were quick to point to their other higher costs (due to their Southern location) limiting their profitability. Thus, it can be concluded that workers who obtained their skills through on-the-job training in general did not emigrate, and so we concentrate only on the possible "backwash effects" on the South due to the migration of graduates of secondary schools and technical institutes.

The South, with 31 percent of the national labor force in 1972, generated 45 percent of the liberal arts graduates, 50 percent of the teachers and 34 percent of the graduates of technical institutes of the nation. Thus, some migration of liberal arts graduates and teachers was essential. That a shortage of technical personnel may not have occurred can be inferred from the following considerations. In 1972, about 2,000 of the 8,000 skilled workers that emigrated from the South went to Rome. Since Rome has practically no industries, it is very likely that these emigrants were liberal arts graduates and teachers who emigrated to Rome to fill civil service jobs. Even if we assume that all the remaining skilled emigrants had technical skills, this would have reduced the supply of technical personnel available to the South from the 1972 graduating class from 59,000 to 53,000 or from 34 to 31 percent of the national total. This figure of 31 percent is to be compared with 31 percent of the total national labor force in the South in 1972, 23 percent of the industrial labor force and 16 percent of the industrial output. Thus, at least on an overall level, no shortage of technical personnel seems to have resulted in the South in 1972 because of emigration. The same general conclusion can be reached for the

[23] *Indagine sui Laureati delle Universita Meridionali nel 1966* (Roma: Censis, 1970).

other years for which data availability makes this calculation possible. However, this is only a tentative conclusion and still leaves the possibility of shortage (due to emigration) in *specific* skills or that, even in the absence of actual shortages, the emigrants represent the most intelligent and best trained people within each skill. These are impossible to prove. But against the latter possibility, the equally reasonable alternative hypothesis must be advanced that the most intelligent and best trained people within each specific occupation do find jobs in the South, while the others unable to find work, eventually decide to emigrate.

From the above analysis, the tentative conclusion can be advanced that emigration did not seem to create labor shortages in the South but represented for the most part resources that would have remained unemployed or underemployed in the South in the absence of migration. The benefit to the South from this migration could then be estimated by the consumption released by emigrants and by the remittances that they sent back to the South.[24] The North also benefitted by avoiding labor shortages.

(b)   South-North capital flow

The above conclusions do not change by examining interregional capital flows between the South and the North of Italy. Empirical evidence covering the period from 1950 to 1974 seems to indicate that the South definitely does not fit into Case 1, but into (what we called before) Case 2 in some years, and Case 3 in others.[25] In the empirical study, most of the attention was focused on bank savings because they represented by far the most important form by which a South-North flow of savings could have occurred in Italy. From the total bank deposits (demand deposits, time deposits and savings deposits) in all banks in the South and the North in each year, the amount which banks in the South and the North had to keep in the form of reserves was deducted. This gave the bank funds available for use in the South and the North in each year. This figure was then compared to the uses (loans and investments) made of bank deposits *within* the South and the North, regardless of the region where these deposits originated.[26]

This comparison showed that during the first eight years (1950–1957) of the 1950–1974 period, the amount of bank funds actually used within the South *exceeded* the sum of bank funds available for use in the South. The difference must have come either from a North-South flow of bank funds or from Southern banks having reserves below their legal reserve requirements and

[24] For a measurement of these effects, see Dominick Salvatore, "The Operation of the Market Mechanism and Regional Inequality," pp. 530–35.

[25] See, Dominick Salvatore, "Interregional Capital Flows and Development," pp. 75–79.

[26] To be noted is that the loans and investments made within the South did not include the loans made at subsidized rates by the special credit institutions created exclusively as part of the development program for the South. The latter were excluded because we were interested in determining whether or not the banking system, *if unregulated,* drained the South of some of its savings.

borrowing from the central bank (or from both sources). A North-South flow of bank funds was particularly likely during the five (of the eight) years when the South had excessive uses of funds over availabilities while the opposite was true in the North. Thus, during these eight years, the Italian South fits into our Case 2.

During sixteen of the remaining seventeen years (1958–1962, 1964–1974), the amount of bank funds available for use in the North and in the South exceeded the amount of bank funds actually used *in both the North and the South*. Thus what we have is Case 3, for these sixteen years. Only in 1963 could a South-North flow of bank funds have taken place. During that year, uses exceeded availability in the North while availability exceeded uses in the South (but was only 23 billion lire).[27] Thus, for the 1950–1974 period taken as a whole, it was concluded that there was a North-South movement of bank funds rather than an opposite movement.

The 9,789 billion lire of *postal* savings raised in Italy (North and South) from 1950 to 1974 was used mostly by the central government (which runs the postal system) to cover its budget deficits incurred primarily to finance the large development program for the South.[28]

Interregional movements of savings via capital markets and through direct investments were much more difficult to ascertain because of lack of adequate data. Whatever information was available, however, seemed to indicate that the South did not suffer a *net* capital outflow through these channels. In Italy, stock ownership—very little widespread in the North—is almost non-existent in the South. Also "It is common knowledge in Italy that municipal bonds have a tendency not to flow out of the area they are issued".[29] In addition, "The direct investments of the residents of the South in the North, are without doubt, barely visible and...it is to be presumed that the direct investments of Northern firms...in the South, were greater than the extremely small investments that Southerners made in the North plus the outflow of interests and profits on previous Northern investments in the South".[30] Most of the investments of Southerners were in real estate purchases in the South, where (because of the rapid expansion of large Southern cities) rents and property values were rising as fast or faster than in the North. Finally, there was an outflow of emigrants' remittances from the North to the South estimated (very conservatively) at about 3,600 billion lire, from 1950 to 1974. Thus it is very likely that the South received a net capital inflow from all these other sources (in addition to a capital inflow through the banking system).

[27] Hence the bulk of the excess of uses of bank funds over their availability in the North, in 1963, must have taken almost entirely the form of Northern banks having reserves below their legal level and borrowing from the bank of Italy.

[28] Banca d'Italia, *Relazioni Annuali 1950–1974* (Roma: Banca d'Italia, 1951–1975) and Amministrazione delle Poste e Telecommunicazioni.

[29] O. Occhiuto and M. Sarcinelli, "Flussi Monetari tra Nord e Sud," *Bollettino* N. 5 (Roma: Banca d'Italia, 1962), p. 578.

[30] Ibid., pp. 577–78.

II. MODELS AND VARIABLES
OF INTERNAL MIGRATION

The type of theoretical and empirical analysis presented before is useful (as far as it goes) but controversial, and economics has long moved toward the development of elaborate theoretical models and very technical empirical estimations in analyzing internal migration as well as almost any other socio-economic event. It is not the purpose of this volume to present in detail and in all of its theoretical and empirical complexities all the models of internal migration available. However, at least a general discussion of these models and variables utilized is essential in order to fully appreciate the simultaneous-equations model that will be developed in the next chapter to analyze the postwar South-North migration in Italy.

1. Time series vs. cross-section models of internal migration

One basic classification of economic models in general and models of internal migration in particular is that between time series and cross section.

(a) Time series models
Time series models analyze how the rate of migration varies over time (usually from year to year) as a result of changes over time in the underlying socio-economic conditions among the regions of a nation. For example, as real wages rise and the rate of unemployment falls in the more developed region relative to the less developed regions over time, we might expect the migration rate from the less developed to the more developed region to rise. On the other hand, if the gap in real wages and unemployment rates narrows between the more developed and the less developed region over time, we might expect the migration rate to decline and possibly even reverse itself. In general, time series analysis is theoretically more appropriate for the analysis of economic relationships. It does, however, present some measurement and practical problems.

One serious econometric problem results because time series of most economic variables tend to move together over time. For example, real industrial wages and the level of real industrial output tend to move up or down together (i.e., to be positively intercorrelated) over time, while real wages and the rate of unemployment tend to be negatively interrelated through time.

The result is that in the econometric estimation of the model, it becomes practically impossible to separate the relative influence or effect of each such intercorrelated variable on the event to be explained or dependent variable.

Another serious econometric problem results because the difference between the actual time series measuring the event to be explained (in our case interregional migration) and the estimated time series, are such that the error term are related over time. This serial correlation of the error term biases our econometric results and generally leads to the underestimation of the significance of each explanatory variable.

Finally, the required time series may not be available or may be available for an inadequate number of years to permit an appropriate econometric estimation of the model. For example, while almost every nation does have yearly data on population, labor force, money wages, prices and rate of unemployment, only few nations have yearly data on internal migration, and only Italy has detailed data on internal *labor* (rather than just population migration) for many years.[1] While advanced econometric techniques exist to correct the problem arising from the temporal intercorrelation of the explanatory variables and error term, the general lack of time series on migration forced most studies on internal migration to use the less appropriate cross-section analysis.

(b) Cross-section models
Cross-section models analyze how the average rate of migration over a year or five years varies as a result of the different socio-economic conditions, distance, climate, etc., exisiting among various regions of a nation *at a particular point in time.* For example, in the Italian context, the migration rate might be higher from Basilicata than from Abruzzo because Abruzzo is relatively better off than Basilicata. The rate of migration might be higher to the richer Northwest than to the Northeast, and to Rome which is less distant and has a better climate than Venice.

Cross-section migration data are generally available from the population censuses conducted by most nations every five or ten years. The difference between two censuses in the number of people living in one region but born in another region gives a rough estimate of the migration between the two census dates. This is only a rough estimate because some migrants may have died, returned to the region of emigration, or emigrated to still other regions between the two censuses, and thus would not be included in the migration figure.

Cross-section analysis of internal migration also face serious econometric problems. Many more variables such as distance and climate which remain the

[1] Italy has collected such data for a variety of socioeconomic reasons (such as the persistent South-North dualism). Only a few other European countries collect yearly data on internal labor migration because of the cost involved and the implied regimentation in maintaining population registers.

14

same over time (and, therefore, are not included in time series analysis) vary among regions and must be included in any cross-section study. The need to include many more variables in cross-section analysis is in itself a problem and also leads to the greater probability that some variable can only be measured qualitatively or not at all.

Another very serious methodological problem facing cross-section studies arises because migration *between* two census dates is postulated to depend on the different socioeconomic conditions existing in the various regions *at the end of the period* (say, the census year). This problem cannot be overcome by also taking an average of the socioeconomic conditions that exist in the various regions between the censuses, because this would imply that such conditions remained constant over time, when in fact they usually vary considerably from year to year.

Since time series analysis is, in general, more appropriate for the estimation of economic relationships, the reason for most migration studies being of a cross-section type is to be found almost exclusively in the general absence of sufficiently long time series on internal migration. Had time series data on internal migration been generally available, the opposite would have been the case. A study on internal migration in Italy thus acquires general importance both because it is only one of few cases where the more appropriate time series analysis of internal migration is possible and also because Italy is a prototype of dualistic development.

2. Single-equation vs. simultaneous-equations models of internal migration

Most migration studies are single-equation because of the great complexity of developing and estimating simultaneous-equation models. However, it is the latter that are clearly required to adequately analyze both the causes of internal migration and its effect on the growth and development of the regions involved and of the nation as a whole.

(a) Single-equation models

Single-equation models, whether time series or cross-section, relate the rate of internal migration to a set of independent or explanatory variables. For example, the rate of migration between the South and the North of Italy might be postulated to depend on the rate of unemployment and real wages in the South and the North. In single-equations models, the causality is unidirectional, running from the independent or explanatory variables to the dependent variable. Thus, the rate of migration is predicted to vary in a specific way depending on the change over time or across regions in the rate of regional unemployment and real wages. No repercussion from the change in the rate of migration on the rate regional unemployment and real wages is possible or acknowledged within these single-equation models. This is clearly inappropriate. If labor migrates from the South because of the lower unemployment rate and

15

higher real wages in the North, then migration by changing the supply and demand of labor both in the South and the North affects the rate of unemployment and real wages in both regions, and that, in turn has repercussions and affects the rate of migration itself. This "single-equation bias" is often very serious but must be balanced against the much greater complexity of setting up and estimating a full-fledged simultaneous-equations model.

Perhaps even more serious is the problem that with single-equation models, only the *causes* of internal migration can be analyzed (more or less adequately). Nothing specific can be inferred from the model itself on the *effects of* migration on the area of emigration, immigration and for the nation as a whole. The effects of migration can only be analyzed within the context of an appropriate simultaneous equations model. In its absence, the discussion of the effects of internal migration often reverts to meaningless, endless and emotional controversy.

(b) Simultaneous-equation models

Simultaneous-equations models, whether time series or cross-section, estimate the effect of a change in one set of variables on another set of variables and then trace the repercussions which a change in the second set of variables has on the first. For example, one equation of the model might postulate internal labor migration (over time or across regions) to depend on the rate of unemployment and real wages in each region. A second equation might postulate that the rate of unemployment in each region might depend on the growth of output and labor force in the region as well as on the rate of labor outmigration or inmigration. Thus, the rate of regional unemployment is at once a determinant of migration (in equation 1) and is itself determined (at least in part) by the rate of migration (in equation 2). A third equation might define the regional real wage rate as dependent explicitly on the rate of unemployment, and indirectly on the rate of labor migration (through the effect that the net labor migration has on the rate of regional unemployment.)

In simultaneous-equations models, one equation is required for each endogenous economic variable, such as the migration rate, the rate of unemployment, and real wages to be determined by the model. Other variables of the model are the exogenous variables determined outside the model and the lagged endogenous variables. It is by its ability to influence these exogenous variables that both the direct as well as the indirect effects of government policies on the endogenous variables of the system can be traced and measured.

How large is a model depends on the function of the model, the availability of data, and the resources at the disposal of the researcher. Some simultaneous equation models have thousands of equations while others have as few as two. While many very large models are being developed and utilized today, there seems also to be a trend toward the better specification of relatively small models. These can outperform much larger, but less carefully specified models.

A simultaneous-equations model of internal migration for Italy is developed and estimated in this study. Not only is this the first time that this is done for Italy but it is the only simultaneous-equations model of internal migration based on time series data.

3. The variables in internal migration models

Ideally, the dependent variable in the migration equation should be the proportion or percentage of the number of *workers* emigrating to the size of the *labor force* in the region of departure. However, because of lack of data, most migration studies use instead the rate of *gross* migration of *people*. In the present study, the theoretically more acceptable net labor migration rate is used as the dependent variable in the migration equation.

The independent or explanatory variables used vary somewhat from study to study. However, they fall into certain broad categories. Practically every study of internal migration (time series as well as cross-section) uses the rate of unemployment and some measure of earnings or wages in the region(s) of emigration and immigration as explanatory variables. Some studies also use the rate of growth of employment opportunities as well as the age of workers. Cross-section studies usually also incorporate distance, the stock of migrants, education, urbanization, and even climate and other sociological regional characteristics as additional explanatory variables. The reason for the inclusion of each of these variables as well as their postulated effect on the rate of internal migration, follows.

(a) Variables in time series and cross-section studies

The rate of unemployment. Practically all studies of internal migration include the rate of unemployment as a crucial explanatory variable. It is postulated that the rate of labor migration is directly related to the rate of unemployment in the (poorer) region of emigration and inversely related to the rate of unemployment in the (richer) region of immigration.

The level of real income or wages. Practically all studies of internal migration also include the level of real income or wages as crucial explanatory variables. Real per capita incomes are often used because of lack of data on real wages. In the present work, the level of real industrial wages is used. It is postulated that the rate of labor migration is inversely related to real wages in the region of departure and directly related to real wages in the area of arrival.

The growth of employment opportunities. The growth of employment opportunities in each region is also sometimes included as a separate explanatory variable because it cannot be inferred that regions with low unemployment rates are also regions of rapidly growing employment opportunities. It is expected that the higher the growth of employment opportunities, the greater the rate of labor immigration or the lower the rate of emigration.

The age of migrants. Age is sometimes included as an explanatory variable, particularly in cross-section studies. It is postulated that the rate of labor migration declines with age since older workers have a shorter expected working life over which to take advantage of the benefits (e.g., the higher earnings) of migration. Furthermore, job security, family and other ties are likely to be stronger for older than for younger workers.

(b) Additional variables in cross-section studies

Distance. The rate of labor migration is postulated to vary inversely with distance. Distance is used as a proxy for the cost of transportation, the psychic costs of migration, as well as for the availability of information.

The stock of migrants. The greater the number of migrants from a particular region, the greater is the amount of information on jobs and socioeconomic conditions usually flowing back to the area of origin. The greater is also the help available to potential migrants among relatives and friends, and, therefore, the greater is the expected rate of migration. This is often referred to as "chain migration" and is usually confirmed by empirical evidence. The corresponding variable in time series studies is the inclusion of the lagged dependent migration variable among the explanatory variables.

Education. It is sometimes postulated that the more educated a worker, the better are his job opportunities, the more information is available to him and the weaker are his family and local ties, and thus the more likely he is to migrate.

Urbanization. For sociological as well as economic reasons, recent decades have witnessed a veritable exodus from rural to urban areas, the world over. Thus, it is postulated that more urbanized regions should attract migrants and more rural regions should lose labor through migration.

Climate and other regional characteristics. Some cross-section studies also use as additional explanatory variables and postulate that regions with better climate, smaller crime rate, less terrorism, etc., are more likely to attract workers.

4. Some representative models of internal migration

(a) A representative time series model

While most migration studies acknowledge that there certainly are many noneconomic forces that also influence internal migration, they invariably postulate internal migration to depend only on some of the socioeconomic variables specified earlier. Empirical results do seem to establish that labor migration be viewed primarily as an *economic* decision. In what follows, some representative migration models will be discussed in general. A more precise and technical presentation of these models is left for the appendices.

One general form of the time series migration model used by the author to analyze the large post-war South-North labor migration in Italy is given by:[2]

---

[2] Dominick Salvatore, "Testing Various Econometric Models of Internal Migration in Italy," *Review of Regional Studies*, VII (1977), pp. 31–41; and Dominick Salvatore, "An Econometric Model of Internal Migration in Italy," *Journal of Regional Science*, XVII (1977), pp. 395–408.

(1) $M_{SNt} = a_0 + a_1 U_{St} + a_2 U_{Nt} + a_3 E_{St} + a_4 E_{Nt} + a_5 W_{St} + a_6 W_{Nt} + a_7 M_{SNt-1}$

where, M_{SNt} = number of workers emigrating from the South to the North in year t as a proportion or percentage of the labor force of the South in year t

U_{St}, U_{Nt} = rate of unemployment in the South and in the North, respectively, in year t

E_{St}, E_{Nt} = rate of growth of the nonagricultural labor force of the South and the North in year t

W_{St}, W_{Nt} = real industrial wage in the South and the North in year t

M_{SNt-1} = rate of South-North labor migration in year t−1

The model postulates that a_1, a_4, a_6 and $a_7 > 0$, while a_2, a_3, $a_5 < 0$. That is, the rate of labor migration between the South and the North in a particular year is directly related to the rate of unemployment in the South in that year, the growth of nonagricultural employment and real industrial wages in the North, and the rate of migration in the previous year. It is inversely related to the rate of unemployment in the North and the growth of nonagricultural employment and real industrial wages in the South. The forces within the South leading to migration are often referred to as the "push forces" of migration. The forces attracting workers to the North are appropriately referred to as "pull forces."

Several aspects of the above model require modification or at least clarification before it can be tested empirically. First, the rate of growth of nonagricultural employment can be expected to be highly intercorrelated with real industrial wages. Both usually rise and fall together in the South and the North. In the empirical estimation of this type of model, it was found that by removing the growth of the nonagricultural employment variables, the overall predictive power of the equation was not reduced, the coefficients remained stable and so these variables were dropped.

Secondly, and for the same reason, the rate of unemployment and real wages *in the South and the North* are likely to rise or fall together. To overcome this problem, either the difference or the ratio in the rate of unemployment and real wages in the South and the North can be used. On theoretical grounds, the difference rather than the ratio of these variables is preferable because workers look at real wage *differences* rather than *ratios* in deciding whether or not to migrate. In this work, both forms were tested and the difference form also performed better empirically. Many migration studies, however, did use the ratio form. In either case, it is then no longer possible to separate the push from the pull forces of migration.

Related to the above is the fact that migrants benefit from higher wages not only in the year of migration but in all the subsequent years of their working life. While most migration studies acknowledge that the *present dis-*

counted value of the real wage difference should be used as an explanatory variable on theoretical grounds, they all invariably go on to use the difference in *current* real wages in their empirical estimation. This is based on the assumption (not entirely unrealistic) that the difference in current real wage rates is a good proxy for present and future real wage differences. This also avoids the controversial choice of discount rates.

Equation (1) can then be rewritten as follows:

$$(2) \qquad M_{SNt} = b_0 + b_1 (U_S - U_N)_t + b_2 (W_S - W_N) + b_3 M_{SNt-1}$$

One important variation of this basic model, attributable to Harris and Todaro,[3] involves weighing the relative real wage difference by the probability of the migrant worker finding employment in the higher real-wage region of immigration (and removing the difference in regional rates of unemployment as a separate explanatory variable). The probability of finding employment is measured by the ratio of the number employed to the total labor force in the region of immigration. Though this may seem attractive, it might still be theoretically better to analyze *separately* the relative effect of the difference in regional unemployment and real wage differences, rather than combine them into a single composite index. Other important variations of the model of equation (2) are presented in Appendix A. The presence of the lagged dependent variable in equation (2) raises serious econometric problems. To overcome these problems, highly sophisticated econometric techniques are required, as shown in Appendix B.

(b) A representative cross-section model

Many of the points raised about single-equation time series models are also pertinent to single-equation, cross-section studies of internal migration, except that many more explanatory variables (not necessary in time series studies) are usually required in these cross-section studies. Most of these cross-section, single-equation models of internal migration are very similar in form. One such typical model by Greenwood, follows:[4]

$$(3) \qquad M_{ij} = f(D_{ij}, Y_{ji}, E_i, E_j, U_i, U_j, R_{ji}, T_{ji}, MS_{ij})$$

where M_{ij} = number of persons, five years of age and over, residing in state j on April 1, 1960, who resided in state i on April 1, 1955, divided by the total number of persons, five years of age and over who resided in state i on April 1, 1955, and in another state on April 1, 1960.

---

[3] J. Harris and H.P. Todaro, "Migration, Unemployment and Development: A Two-Sector Analysis," *American Economic Review*, LX (1970), pp. 126–42.

[4] Michael J. Greenwood, "An Analysis of the Determinants of Geographic Labor Mobility in the United States," *Review of Economics and Statistics*, LI (1969), pp. 189–94.

D_{ij} = 1955 highway mileage between the principal city of state i and that of state j.

Y_{ji} = median 1959 money income of males living in state j in 1960 divided by the median 1959 money income of males living in state i in 1960.

E_i = median number of years of school completed by residents of state i, 25 years of age and over, 1960.

E_j = median number of years of school completed by residents of state j, 25 years of age and over, 1960.

U_i = percent of the civilian labor force unemployed in state i during approximately the first week of April, 1960.

U_j = percent of the civilian labor force unemployed in state j during approximately the first week of April, 1960.

R_{ji} = percent of population living in urban areas of state j in 1960 divided by the percent of population living in urban areas of state i in 1960.

T_{ji} = mean yearly temperature in the principal city of state j divided by the mean yearly temperature in the principal city of state i.

MS_{ij} = number of persons born in state i and living in state j, 1950.

Greenwood postulates that M_{ij} is directly related to Y_{ji}, E_i, U_i, R_{ji}, T_{ji}, MS_{ij} and indirectly related to D_{ij}, E_j and U_j. Note how this type of model involves more variables than are required in a time series model of the type given in equation (2), and how it treats the variables in a less symmetrical way. A cross-section model of this type was necessitated by lack of time series data on internal migration in the United States. However, this model is theoretically less elegant and its empirical performance is inferior and more controversial when compared to the time series models developed and tested for the Italian case by the author.

Since theory does not specify the form of the relationship, these models can be estimated in linear, semilog, inverse semilog or double log form. Estimation in double log form (as Greenwood did in the model presented above) is attractive because the coefficients measure elasticities.

In the empirical estimation of these time series and cross-section models, most of the variable included have the right sign and are often statistically significant.[5] However, they are all subject to single-equation bias in estimation and thus view internal migration in a far too restrictive framework which precludes the analysis of important policy questions. A simultaneous-equation model for Italy using time series data will be developed in the next chapter. A typical cross-section simultaneous-equations model of internal migration is presented in Appendix C.

---

[5] See the articles themselves for these empirical results.

21

III. A SIMULTANEOUS EQUATIONS MODEL OF INTERNAL MIGRATION IN ITALY

1. The background

Since the end of World War II, the rate of growth in the labor force has been much greater in the South than in the North, while the expansion of employment opportunities has been much larger in the North. This resulted in a large labor migration from the South to the North and to foreign nations.[1] Even so, the rate of unemployment has remained significantly higher in the South than in the North since the early 1950s. It is safe to assume that in the absence of labor migration, the rate of unemployment in the South would have been significantly greater throughout the period. At the same time, the level of real wages in the modern industrial and service sectors of the South have risen significantly over time and have generally kept pace with the rise in real wages in the North.

(a) The economy of the South

In view of what has been said above, the South can be regarded as an economy in disequilibrium and can be analyzed with the aid of Fig. 1.

In Fig. 1, D_L and S_L refer to the demand and supply curve of labor, respectively, in the modern urban sector of the South, before internal and foreign labor migration. W* refers to the (above equilibrium) negotiated real wages in the modern urban sector of the South, and U* to its level of urban unemployment at W*.

At W*, U* tends to rise as S_L shifts to the right through natural increases in the labor force of the South and from rural-urban labor migration within the South. U* tends to fall as S_L shifts to the left as a result of the net South-North labor migration and from the net South-foreign labor migration.[2] U* also tends

---

[1] The net labor migration from the North to foreign nations has been significantly less than for the South and occurred not because of lack of employment opportunities in the North but primarily in response to higher wages in the more highly industrialized nations such as Germany and the United States.

[2] It might be argued that labor migration reduces not only the supply of labor in the South but also the demand for labor by eliminating the demand for goods and services of the emigrants. However, in a labor-surplus economy as the South, most of the effect of labor migration on labor markets can be expected to come from the supply side rather than from the demand side, and reduce the rate of unemployment. Similarly, the natural increase in the labor force of the South can be expected to increase unemployment in the South in the absence of migration.

Figure 1. Modern Urban Labor Market in the South

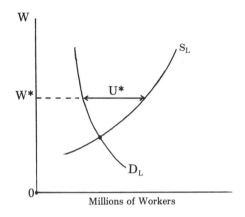

Millions of Workers

to fall as D_L shifts to the right due to increases in urban real value added in the South. These forces affecting regional labor demand and supply are reflected in equation (2) in the next section.

Urban real wages in the South are restrained from rising further (above their equilibrium level) by rising unemployment rates and the high proportion of the regional labor force ready to leave agriculture. In this disequilibrium model, the growth of real value added in the urban modern sector of the South affects urban real wages only indirectly, through its effect on the rate of regional unemployment. This is reflected in equation (4) in the next section.

Since there seemed to have been a surplus not only of labor in general but also of skilled labor in the South, before and after migration throughout the period of the analysis (see Section 3 in Chapter I), the growth of urban real value added was crucially dependent only on the level of net regional investments and technological progress. Net investments in the South have been supplemented by large and continuous North-South capital transfer as part of the development program for the South. Since this North-South capital transfer depended on the political process, and technological progress is taken as exogenous, the growth of real urban output is taken as exogenous in this model.[3]

(b) The economy of the North
The economy of the North is generally more efficient than the economy of the

---

[3] Rising real urban wages above productivity increases, lead to excessive capital-intensive production techniques which reduce the growth of urban employment, as reflected in the wage elasticity of the demand for labor in the South in Figure 1.

South and more closely resembles the economy of highly developed nations.[4] The proportion of the labor force employed in Northern agriculture is today less than half that of the South. In addition, Northern agriculture is relatively efficient and market oriented while that of the South traditional and subsistence. As a result, the degree of dualism between industry and agriculture and modern and traditional is much less in the North than in the South.

During the post-war period, employment opportunities in the North grew relatively much faster than the natural growth of its labor force and was able to provide employment for the more than one million workers that emigrated from the South, at rapidly rising real wages and with low rates of regional unemployment. Not being in disequilibrium, an analysis of labor markets in the North is significantly different from the analysis of labor markets in the South (which are in disequilibrium).

In the rapidly growing and dynamic economy of the North, the growth of the regional labor force as well as the net labor migration from the South prevented labor shortages and was an important stimulus to continued rapid growth. Thus, while the excessive natural growth of the labor force tended to increase the rate of unemployment in the labor-surplus economy of the South, the growth of the labor force stimulated the economy of the North and tended to reduce the Northern rate of unemployment. Similarly, the South-North net labor migration can be expected to reduce the rate of unemployment in the North, while labor migration from the North to foreign nations can be expected to increase it.[5] These forces, together with the growth of real industrial output in the North, are reflected in equation (3) in the next section and are clearly and strongly confirmed by the empirical results presented in Chapter IV.

As in the South, real wages in the North can be expected to be inversely related to the rate of unemployment in the North. Furthermore, because of strong labor unions, real wages in the modern sector are expected to rise each year by a negotiated amount over past real wages. Thus, real wages in the previous period are included as an explanatory variable of the level of current real wages. Since in the North, the agricultural sector is relatively less important and more efficient and commercial than in the South, the proportion of the labor force in agriculture in the North is not included as a separate explanatory variable in the wage equation of the North as was done for the South. These forces are reflected in equation (5) in the next section.

The rate of net labor migration from the South to the North is then postulated to depend on the difference in the rates of regional unemployment

[4] To be sure, the North is not uniformly developed and efficient. For example, the Northwest includes the more dynamic industrial triangle, while the Northeast and Center share some of the economic characteristics of the South. However, it is perhaps safe to conclude that the least dynamic areas of the North may be comparable to the most efficient and rapidly growing of the South.

[5] See, R. Muth, "Migration: Chicken or Egg," *Southern Economic Journal,* XXXVII (1971), pp. 295–306.

and real wages between the South and the North. This is reflected in equation (1) (the migration equation) in the next section.

(c) Additional observations

If, as postulated above, the net South-North labor migration reduces the rate of regional unemployment in both the South and the North (in the South, by reducing the supply of surplus labor, and in the North, by further stimulating growth), it would then benefit both the South and the North. This would confirm the neoclassical analysis of Chapter I and refute the analysis of Myrdal and Hirschman. It would, however, be impossible to determine on theoretical grounds the effect that this South-North net labor migration would have on South-North regional differences. This would depend on the relative decline in the rate of regional unemployment and (through it) on the relative rise in regional real wages in the South and the North.

If the net South-North labor migration caused a greater absolute decline in the rate of unemployment and a greater absolute increase in real wages in the South than in the North, South-North differences would decline. Otherwise, they would remain unchanged or rise. This important question can only be answered on the basis of the size of the actual coefficients obtained in the empirical estimation in Chapter IV.

Even if regional inequalities were to rise when both the South and the North benefit from labor migration, this should be viewed as quite different from the case where regional differences rose because net labor migration was detrimental to the South. An increase in regional differences resulting from the South benefitting less than the North from the net South-North labor migration is an important result in and of itself since it would still justify an even greater national development effort for the South, financed primarily from some of the benefit accruing to the North from the net labor migration from the South. This would also serve to compensate the South for the heavy burden of raising, educating and training workers who then migrate and benefit the North.

Nor can continued South-North net labor migration and persistent or even increasing regional differences in rates of unemployment and real wages be regarded as evidence that labor markets are not operating or are functioning perversely, because in the absence of migration, regional differences might (and would probably) be even greater than they are presently. In short, the South is an economy in *dynamic* disequilibrium where excessive natural growth of the labor force continues to supply more labor than can effectively be utilized within the South and is constantly generating a surplus of labor. The net labor migration from the South to the North and to foreign nations only prevented such labor surplus and unemployment rate in the South from becoming much larger. It is only as socioeconomic conditions improve sufficiently in the South over time and with a sustained and increased development effort that we can expect the demand for labor in the South to catch up with the natural increase in its labor force and the serious disequilibrium in its labor markets be eliminated.

2. The formal model

The formal model presented in this section postulates that internal labor migration in Italy can be viewed primarily as a response to the significant socioeconomic differences between the South and the North. These are reflected in a higher present and expected unemployment rate and lower real wages in the South than in the North. However, net internal labor migration affects the supply and demand of labor and thus the rate of unemployment and real wages in both the South and the North. Since internal labor migration is postulated to depend primarily on the difference in expected unemployment rates and real wages, a simultaneous equations model must be developed which allows for their simultaneous determination.

The model presented below consists of five first-order difference equations, determining the rate of net labor migration from the South to the North and the rate of unemployment and real wage in the South and in the North.[6]

(1) $\quad M_{SNt} = a_0 + a_1 U_{St} + a_2 U_{Nt} + a_3 W_{St} + a_4 W_{Nt} + a_5 D + a_6 M_{SNt-1}$

(2) $\quad U_{St} = b_0 + b_1 M_{SNt} + b_2 M_{SFt} + b_3 Q_{St} + b_4 L_{St} + b_5 U_{St-1}$

(3) $\quad U_{Nt} = c_0 + c_1 M^*_{SNt} + c_2 M_{NFt} + c_3 Q_{Nt} + c_4 L_{Nt} + c_5 U_{Nt-1}$

(4) $\quad W_{St} = d_0 + d_1 U_{St} + d_2 A_{St} + d_3 W_{St-1}$

(5) $\quad W_{Nt} = e_0 + e_1 U_{Nt} + e_2 W_{Nt-1}$

where, M_{SNt} = net number of workers emigrating from the South to the North in year t, as a percentage of the labor force of the South.

M^*_{SNt} = net number of workers emigrating from the South to the North in year t, *as percentage of the labor force of the North.*

M_{SFt}, M_{NFt} = net number of workers emigrating from the South and the North *to foreign nations* in year t, as a percentage of the labor force of the South and the North.

U_{St}, U_{Nt} = average unemployment rate in the South and the North in year t.

W_{St}, W_{Nt} = average wages per employed worker in industry in the South and the North in year t, expressed in 100,000 lire, deflated by the consumer price index.

---

[6] Real industrial wages and the growth of real value added in industry were used in the empirical estimation of the model as a proxy for real urban wages and the growth of urban real value added. In Italy, industry is broadly defined to include construction and is regarded as the leading sector in creating more jobs. In addition, real wages in the service sector closely follow industrial wages and most of the labor migrating to the North goes into industry.

D = dummy variable taking the value of 1 for the year 1961 (when the unregistered migrants to the North of previous years were allowed to register) and zero in other years.

Q_{St}, Q_{Nt} = percentage growth of real value added in industry in the South and the North in year t.

L_{St}, L_{Nt} = percentage growth in the labor force of the South and the North, respectively, in year t.

A_{St} = percentage of the labor force employed in agriculture in the South in year t.

The introduction of the lagged dependent as an explanatory variable in all stochastic equations gives the model its dynamic structure. It results from taking all exogenous variables as expected values, with expectations generally formed on the basis of a distributed lag of current and past values of the exogenous variables.

3. Elaboration of the model

In equation (1), it is postulated that a_1, a_4, a_5, $a_6 > 0$, while a_2 and $a_3 < 0$. That is, net labor migration from the South to the North in a given year is directly related to the rate of unemployment in the South in the same year, to real wages in the North in that year, a dummy variable that allowed the unregistered labor migrants to the North of previous years to register in 1961,[7] and to the rate of migration in the previous year. As pointed out in Chapter II, the migration of labor from a particular region of the South to the North in a given year can be expected to stimulate and facilitate additional migration from the region in the subsequent year. On the other hand, net labor migration from the South to the North in a given year is inversely related to the rate of unemployment in the North and to real wages in the South in the same year.

In equation (2), it is postulated that b_1, b_2, $b_3 < 0$, while b_4 and $b_5 > 0$. That is, the rate of unemployment in the South in a particular year is inversely related to the rate of net labor migration from the South to the North and to foreign nations during the same year, and to the growth of real value added in the South during that year. On the other hand, the rate of unemployment in the South in a given year is directly related to the natural growth of its labor force and to the rate of unemployment in the South in the previous year. Thus, the rate of unemployment in the South falls as labor migrates to the North and to foreign nations and as its real industrial output rises, and rises as its labor

---

[7] This inflated the 1961 *recorded* South-North net labor migration by about 20-30 percent. To be pointed out is that in my previous econometric work on internal migration in Italy in the *Review of Regional Studies* and the *Journal of Regional Science* in 1977, a dummy variable was used for 1961 and 1962. However, the results presented in Chapter IV are very similar whether a dummy is used only for 1961 or for 1961 and 1962.

force increases. Variable L (the natural growth of labor force) is measured *before* migration and reflects not only new entrants into and departures from the labor force at retirement age but also changes in the participation rate (which, as it will be seen later, declined significantly over the period of the analysis in both the South and the North).

In equation (3), it is expected that c_1, c_3, $c_4 < 0$, while c_2 and $c_5 > 0$. That is, the rate of unemployment in the North in a given year is postulated to be inversely related to the rate of net labor migration from the South, to the growth of industrial output in the North, and to the natural increase in the labor force of the North during the same year. On the other hand, the rate of unemployment in the North during a given year is expected to be directly related to the rate of net labor migration from the North to foreign nations in the same year and to the rate of unemployment in the North in the previous year. As pointed out in the previous section, the net increase in the supply of labor of the North resulting from the net labor migration from the South and from the natural increase in the labor force of the North, prevent labor shortages and stimulate growth in the North, and thus can be expected to reduce its unemployment rate. On the other hand, the labor migration from the North to foreign nations, by reducing the supply of labor in the North, reduces its rate of growth and can be expected to increase its rate of unemployment. Note that the net migration of labor from the South to the North is expected to be inversely related to the rate of unemployment both in the South and in the North (i.e., b_1 and c_1 in equation 2 and 3, respectively, are both expected to have a negative sign).

In equation (4), W_{St} is expected to be inversely related to U_{St} and A_{St} but directly related to W_{St-1} (i.e., d_1 and $d_2 < 0$, while $d_3 > 0$). That is, the higher the rate of unemployment and the proportion of the labor force in agriculture in the South in a particular year, and the lower the real wage rate in the South in the previous year, the lower is the real wage rate of the South this year expected to be. As pointed out in the previous section, the high percentage of labor in agriculture in the South, ready to move as soon as the opportunity for non-agricultural jobs arises, is expected to be a deterrent to rising industrial wages even in the face of a relatively low and unchanging averge unemployment rate in the region. Furthermore, Q_{St} affects W_{St} only indirectly, through its effect on U_{St}.

In equation (5), W_{Nt} is expected to be inversely related to U_{Nt} but directly related to W_{Nt-1} (i.e., $e_1 < 0$, while $e_2 > 0$). That is, the lower the rate of unemployment in the North in a particular year and the higher the real wages of the North in the previous year, the higher the real wages of the North this year are expected to be. Note that the proportion of the labor force in agriculture in the North is not included as an independent explanatory variable for the real wage rate in the North (as it was done for the South in equation 4). The reason for this is that, as pointed out earlier, the proportion of the labor force in agriculture in the North is small absolutely and less than half that of the South. More importantly, is the fact that Northern agriculture is relatively much more efficient and rewarding than that of the South and so labor is not as eager and ready to move out of agriculture and into industry as in the South. Finally, as in the case of the South in equation (4), Q_{Nt} affects W_{Nt} only indirectly, through its effect on U_{Nt}.

4. Summarizing the model

Summarizing briefly the inherent logic of the model as a whole, it can be seen in equation (2) that changes in the rate of net labor migration from the South to the North and to foreign nations, and in the natural growth rate of the labor force and industrial output in the South, affect the rate of unemployment in the South. A change in the rate of net labor migration from the South to the North (as a percentage of the labor force of the North), in the net rate of labor migration from the North to foreign nations, and in the natural growth rate of the labor force and industrial output in the North, affect the rate of unemployment in the North (equation 3).

A change in the rate of unemployment and in the proportion of the labor force employed in agriculture in the South, affect the real wage rate in the South (equation 4). A change in the rate of unemployment in the North affects the real wage rate in the North (equation 5).

Changes in the rate of unemployment and real wages in the South and in the North affect the rate of net labor migration from the South to the North (equation 1) which, in turn, affects the rate of unemployment in the South and in the North and, through them, the real wage rate in the South and the North, respectively.

This is a simultaneous-equations model in the sense that a change in any part of the system has repercussions and affects every other part of the system. For example, an autonomous increase in the rate of growth of industrial output in the South tends to reduce the rate of unemployment in the South (equation 2) and through it, to increase real industrial wages in the South (equation 3). These reduce the net South-North labor migration rate which, in turn, tends to increase the rate of unemployment in both the South and the North and, through them, to reduce real wages in both the South and the North. These changes in the rate of unemployment and real wages in both the South and the North then affect the South-North net labor migration. The process continues until all the repercussions have worked themselves out.

The simultaneous aspect of the model discussed above is presented schematically in Fig. 2. The process is assumed to begin with an autonomous change in Q_{St} and arrows indicate causality.

Figure 2. Simultaneity in the Model

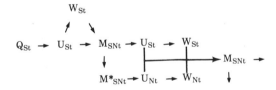

APPENDICES

APPENDIX A

TIME SERIES MODELS
OF INTERNAL MIGRATION

The author tested a static expectations, dynamic expectations, extrapolative expectations, and information flow model for South-North migration in Italy.[1] The variables used in the study were:

M_{SNt} = net number of *workers* emigrating from the South to the North during year t, per 1,000 of the labor force of the South

$U_t = (U_S - U_N)_t$ or $\left(\frac{U_S}{U_N}\right)_t =$ difference or ratio in the average unemployment rate in year t between the South and the North

$E_t = (E_S - E_N)_t$ or $\left(\frac{E_S}{E_N}\right)_t =$ difference or ratio in the average nonagricultural employment growth in year t between the South and the North

$W_t = (W_S - W_N)_t$ or $\left(\frac{W_S}{W_N}\right)_t =$ difference or ratio in the average real industrial wage in year t between the South and the North

$Y_t = (Y_S - Y_N)_t$ or $\left(\frac{Y_S}{Y_N}\right)_t =$ difference or ratio in the average real income of employed workers in year t between the South and the North

$D =$ dummy variable to take into consideration the change in the migration law which occurred in Feb. 1961

---

[1] For a theoretical discussion and empirical results of these models, see Dominick Salvatore, "Testing Various Econometric Models of Internal Migration in Italy," *Review of Regional Studies,* VII (1977), p. 31–41. Reprinted by permission of the *Review of Regional Studies.*

The form of the models was:

Static Expectations:
(1) $M_{SNt} = \alpha_0 + \alpha_1 U_t + \alpha_2 E_t + \alpha_3 W_t + \alpha_4 D + e_t$

Dynamic Expectations:
(2) $M_{SNt} = \beta_0 + \beta_1 U_t + \beta_2 E_t + \beta_3 W_5 + \beta_4 M_{SNt-1} + \beta_5 D + v_t$

Extrapolative Expectations:
(3) $M_{SNt} = \delta_0 + \delta_1 U_t^* + \delta_2 E_t^* + \delta_3 W_t^* + \delta_4 D + u_t$ where
(4) $U_t^* = U_t + \lambda(U_t - U_{t-1}) = U_t + \lambda \Delta U_t$
The same is true for E_t^* and W_t^*, so that we get:
(5) $M_{SNt} = \delta_0 + \delta_1 U_t + \delta_1 \lambda \Delta U_t + \delta_2 E_t + \delta_2 \lambda \Delta E_t + \delta_3 W_t + \delta_3 \lambda \Delta W_t + \delta_4 D$
$\quad + u_t$

Information Flow:
(6) $M_{SNt} = \theta_0 + \theta_1 U_t + \theta_2 E_t + \theta_3 W_t + \theta_4 MS_t + \theta_5 D + \varepsilon_t$ where

MS_t = stock of migrant workers from the South residing in the North in year t

Previous migrants send information back home on opportunities in the North and generally facilitate further migration from the South. We do not have annual MS_t data, but setting M_{SNt-1} equal to $MS_t - MS_{t-1}$, we can specify this information flow model as:

(7) $M_{SNt} = \theta_1 \Delta U_t + \theta_2 \Delta E_t + \theta_3 \Delta W_t + \theta_4 M_{SNt-1} + \theta_5 D + \eta_t$

Equation (7) will also be estimated with a constant term [which is equivalent to including a time trend in (7)].

APPENDIX B

ECONOMETRIC NOTES
ON THE ESTIMATION OF
A DYNAMIC TIME SERIES MODEL
OF INTERNAL MIGRATION

Of the models presented in Appendix A, the dynamic expectations model (with the variables measured in difference form and with variable E dropped —see the discussion in Chapter II) is better theoretically and also performs better empirically. However, that model faces serial correlation. A more rigorous reformulation of the dynamic expectations model presented in Appendix A as well as the steps to overcome the serial correlation problem is given below:[1]

(1) $$M_{ijt} = a_0 + a_1 U^*_{it} + a_2 U^*_{jt} + a_3 W^*_{it} + a_4 W^*_{jt}$$

(2) $$M_{jit} = a_0' + a_1' U^*_{it} + a_2' U^*_{jt} + a_3' W^*_{it} + a_4' W^*_{jt}$$

(3) $$N_{ijt} = (a_0 - a_0') + (a_1 - a_1') U^*_{it} + (a_2 - a_2') U^*_{jt}$$
$$+ (a_3 - a_3') W^*_{it} + (a_4 - a_4') W^*_{jt}$$

where, M_{ijt} refers to the gross migration rate of workers from region i to region j in period t, N_{ijt} refers to the net migration rate from i to j in period t, U^*_{it} and U^*_{jt} refer, respectively, to the expected unemployment rate in region i and j in period t, and W^*_{it} and W^*_{jt} refer, respectively, to the expected real wage rate in region i and j in period t.

If it is assumed that migration in year t is a function of the expected values of U and W and these expectations are generally formed on the basis of a distributed lag of current and past values of the explanatory variables, we can then postulate a general distributed lag model which states that N_{ijt} is partly determined by its own value in the previous period and partly by the actual exogenous variables, and with the disturbance term autocorrelated with a first-order autoregressive scheme

---

[1] For a more detailed discussion of the model and for the empirical results for its application to the labor migration from each of the regions of the South to the Northwest and to the North as a whole, see Dominick Salvatore, "An Econometric Model of Internal Migration in Italy," *Journal of Regional Science*, XVII (1977), pp. 395–408. Reprinted by permission of the *Journal of Regional Science*.

(4) $$N_{ijt} = b_0 + b_1 U_{it} + b_2 U_{jt} + b_3 W_{it} + b_4 W_{jt} + b_5 N_{ijt-1} + e_t$$

where $b_k = (a_k - a_k')$ for $k = 0, 1, \cdots 4$, and $e_t = \varrho e_{t-1} + v_t$ with $|\varrho| < 1$ and v's NID $(0, \sigma_v^2)$.

However, Equation (4) violates two basic assumptions of OLS, since

(5) $$E(e_t N_{ijt-1}) \neq 0 \text{ and } E(e_t e_{t-1}) \neq 0$$

Violation of these assumptions results in biased and inconsistent estimates and renders OLS inappropriate. To deal with both of these problems, the Wallis method is used. This is a combination of instrumental variables (to tackle the first problem) and GLS adjusted for bias (to tackle the second problem). In our case, this involves the following practical steps

First, regress N_{ijt} on all the actual exogenous variables in period t using OLS

(6) $$N_{ijt} = c_0 + c_1 U_{it} + c_2 U_{jt} + c_3 W_{it} + c_4' W_{jt} + v_t$$

Second, use the estimated coefficients to form the regression estimate and lag this one period, giving $\hat{N}_{ijt-1}$, a linear combination of the exogenous variables. $\hat{N}_{ijt-1}$ is then used as an instrumental variable in (7)

(7) $$N_{ijt} = c_0' + c_1' U_{it} + c_2' U_{jt} + c_3' W_{it} + c_4' W_{jt} + c_5' \hat{N}_{ijt-1} + e_t$$

Thirdly, from the regression residuals in (7), calculate the first order serial correlation coefficient, making a correction for bias

(8) $$r = [\textstyle\sum_{t=2}^{n} \hat{e}_t \hat{e}_{t-1}/(n-1)]/[\textstyle\sum_{t=1}^{n} \hat{e}_t^2/n] + (6/n)$$

Finally, using r as an estimate of ϱ, calculate Aitken's GLS of the coefficients

(9) $$\begin{aligned}(N_{ijt} - \varrho N_{ijt-1}) = c_0^* &+ c_1^*(U_{it} - \varrho U_{it-1}) + c_2^*(U_{jt} - \varrho U_{jt-1}) \\ &+ c_3^*(W_{it} - \varrho W_{it-1}) + c_4^*(W_{jt} - \varrho W_{jt-1}) \\ &+ c_5^*(N_{ijt-1} - \varrho N_{ijt-2}) + e_t^*\end{aligned}$$

Wallis showed that his estimate of the c^*'s are consistent and asymptotically efficient and are much better than the OLS estimator applied directly to (4), to the instrumental variable estimator and to the three-pass least-squares method suggested by Taylor and Wilson.

APPENDIX C

A CROSS-SECTION MODEL
OF INTERNAL MIGRATION

An example of a cross-section simultaneous-equations model of internal labor migration in the United States is provided by Greenwood.[1] In the model CLF refers to the current labor force and "^" to predicted values. The basic model estimated for the study consists of 14 equations (nine structural and five identities) in 14 jointly dependent (endogenous) variables. The endogenous variables include the rate of CLF out-migration (OM), the rate of CLF in-migration (IM), the rate of income growth (ΔINC), the rate of employment growth (ΔEMP), the rate of unemployment growth (ΔUNEMP), the rate of natural growth of the CLF (NATINC), and the rate of total CLF growth (ΔCLF). Out-migration is disaggregated to out-migration to other SMSA's (OMTS) and out-migration to nonmetropolitan areas (OMTN). In-migration is disaggregated to in-migration from other SMSA's (IMFS) and in-migration from nonmetropolitan areas (IMFN). Finally, employment growth is disaggregated into component changes in manufacturing employment (ΔMANU), government employment (ΔGEMP), and other nonmanufacturing employment (ΔNMANU). All changes relating to CLF variables are expressed relative to the beginning-of-period CLF level so as to allow formation of the identities that close the model. Specifically, the model is of the following form:

$$\text{OMTS} = f_1(\widehat{\text{IMFS}}, \Delta \text{IN}\widehat{\text{C}}, \Delta \widehat{\text{EMP}}, \Delta \text{UN}\widehat{\text{EMP}}, \text{INC}, \text{UNR},$$
$$\text{CLF}, \text{EDU}, \text{AGE}, D1, D2, D3, D4, e_1); \tag{2.1}$$

$$\text{OMTN} = f_2(\widehat{\text{IMFN}}, \cdots, e_2); \tag{2.2}$$

$$\text{IMFS} = f_2(\widehat{\text{OMTS}}, \Delta \text{IN}\widehat{\text{C}}, \Delta \text{E}\widehat{\text{MP}}, \Delta \text{UN}\widehat{\text{EMP}}, \text{INC},$$
$$\text{UNR}, \text{CLF}, D1, D2, D3, D4, e_3); \tag{2.3}$$

$$\text{IMPN} = f_4(\widehat{\text{OMTN}}, \cdots, e_4); \tag{2.4}$$

[1]For a theoretical discussion of this model and the empirical results, see Michael Greenwood, "A Simultaneous-Equations Model of Urban Growth and Migration," *Journal of the American Statistical Association*, LXX (1975), pp. 798–810. Reprinted by permission of the *Journal of the American Statistical Association*.

$$\Delta\text{INC} = f_5(\hat{\text{OM}}, \hat{\text{IM}}, \text{NA}\hat{\text{T}}\text{INC}, \Delta\text{UN}\hat{\text{E}}\text{MP}, \text{INC},$$
$$\Delta\text{EDU}, \%\text{NW}, \Delta\text{ARMFC}, D1, D2, D3,$$
$$D4, e_5); \tag{2.5}$$

$$\Delta\text{MANU} = f_6(\hat{\text{OM}}, \hat{\text{IM}}, \text{NA}\hat{\text{T}}\text{INC}, \text{MANU}, \text{INC}, \text{RRET},$$
$$\Delta\text{EDU}, \Delta\text{ARMFC}, D1, D2, D3, D4, e_6); \tag{2.6}$$

$$\Delta\text{GEMP} = f_7(\hat{\text{OM}}, \hat{\text{IM}}, \text{NA}\hat{\text{T}}\text{INC}, \Delta\hat{\text{I}}\text{NC}, \text{GEMP}, \Delta\text{EDU},$$
$$\Delta\text{ARMFC}, D1, D2, D3, D4, e_7); \tag{2.7}$$

$$\Delta\text{NMANU} = f_8(\hat{\text{OM}}, \hat{\text{IM}}, \text{NA}\hat{\text{T}}\text{INC}, \Delta\text{MA}\hat{\text{N}}\text{U}, \text{NMANU},$$
$$\text{INC}, \Delta\text{EDU}, \Delta\text{ARMFC}, D1, D2, D3, D4, e_8); \tag{2.8}$$

$$\Delta\text{UNEMP} = f_9(\hat{\text{OM}}, \hat{\text{IM}}, \text{NA}\hat{\text{T}}\text{INC}, \Delta\hat{\text{I}}\text{NC}, \text{UNR}, \%\text{NW},$$
$$\Delta\text{ARMFC}, D1, D2, D3, D4, e_9); \tag{2.9}$$

$$\text{OM} \equiv \text{OMTS} + \text{OMTN}; \tag{2.10}$$

$$\text{IM} \equiv \text{IMFS} + \text{IMFN}; \tag{2.11}$$

$$\Delta\text{CLF} \equiv \Delta\text{EMP} + \Delta\text{UNEMP}; \tag{2.12}$$

$$\Delta\text{EMP} \equiv \Delta\text{MANU} + \Delta\text{GEMP} + \Delta\text{NMANU}; \tag{2.13}$$

$$\text{NATING} \equiv \Delta\text{CLF} + \text{OM} - \text{IM}. \tag{2.14}$$

APPENDIX D

ECONOMETRIC NOTES ON THE ESTIMATION OF THE SIMULTANEOUS-EQUATION TIME SERIES MODEL OF INTERNAL MIGRATION

Each of the five equations of the model presented in Chapter II are over-identified because the number of variables excluded from each equation exceeds four.

TSLS estimation can be summarized as follows:[1]

The ith structural equation of the general model can be written as:

$$y_i = a_{i1}y_1 + a_{i2}y_2 + \cdots + a_{iG}y_G + b_{i1}x_1 + \cdots + b_{ik}x_k + u_i$$

where, y_i's = endogenous variables (i = 1, 2, ... G)

x_i's = predetermined variables (i = 1, 2, ... k)

a's = coefficients of endogenous variables

b's = coefficients of predetermined variables.

In the first stage, we apply OLS to the reduced-form equations to obtain estimates of the c's:

$$y_1 = c_{11}x_1 + c_{12}x_2 + \ldots + c_{1k}x_k + v_1$$
$$y_2 = c_{21}x_1 + c_{22}x_2 + \ldots + c_{2k}x_k + v_2$$

$$\vdots$$

$$y_G = c_{G1}x_1 + c_{G2}x_2 + \ldots + c_{Gk}x_k + v_G$$

using the reduced form coefficients, $\hat{c}$'s, we obtain $\hat{y}_1, \hat{y}_2, \ldots, \hat{y}_G$.

In the second stage, we substitute the $\hat{y}$'s into the structural equation and obtain the transformed functions:

$$y_i = a_{i1}\hat{y}_1 + a_{i2}\hat{y}_2 + \ldots + a_{iG}\hat{y}_G + b_{i1}x_1 + \ldots + b_{ik}x_k + u_i^*$$

where, $\qquad u_i^* = u_i + a_{i1}v_1 + a_{i2}v_2 + \ldots + a_{iG}v_G$

[1] R. Bausmann, "A Generalized Classical Method of Linear Estimation of Coefficients in a Structural Equation," *Econometrica*, XXV (1957), pp. 77–83.

Serial correlation of the error terms was removed by:[2]

$$y^*_{it} = a_{i1}(1-\varrho)\hat{y}^*_{1t} + a_{i2}(1-\varrho)\hat{y}^*_{2t} + \ldots + a_{iG}(1-\varrho)\hat{y}^*_{Gt} + b_{i1}(1-\varrho)x^*_{it} +$$
$$\ldots + b_{ik}(1-\varrho)x^*_{kt} + e_{it}$$

where, $y^*_{it} = y_{it} - \varrho y_{it-1}$
$x^*_{it} = x_{it} - \varrho x_{it-1}$
$e_{it} = u^*_{it} - \varrho u^*_{it-1}$
ϱ = the scanning algorithm (from -1.0 to 1.0 at 0.05 intervals) which gives the lowest transformed error sum of squares.

The stability and steady state equilibrium of the model was analyzed by finding solutions to the characteristic equation.[3] All characteristic roots but one are less than one in magnitude and have no imaginary component. One of them, however, is greater than one and introduces some instability into the model. This only made possible the measurement of the impact or short-run results of the various policies analyzed in Chapter IV instead of their long-run effects.

In the simulation, the Newton method was used.[4]

The formula and interpretation of Theil's inequality coefficient (T) is as follows:[5]

$$T = \frac{\sqrt{1/n\ \Sigma(P_i - A_i)^2}}{\sqrt{1/n\ \Sigma P_i^2} + \sqrt{1/n\ \Sigma A_i^2}}$$

where, P = predicted value
A = actual value
n = the sample size

Thus, the numerator is the RMSE and the denominator represents weights which constrain the value of T to $0 \leqslant T \leqslant 1$. The closer the value of t is to zero, the better are the results of the dynamic historical simulation. A particular value of T can be decomposed into three proportions:

$$\frac{\overline{P} - \overline{A}}{D} + \frac{s_P - s_A}{D} + \frac{\sqrt{2(1-r)s_P s_A}}{D} = 1$$ where, P, A, s_p, s_A are the means

and standard deviations of series P_i and A_i, respectively, and r is the correlation coefficient, while D is the denominator in T. These give, respectively, the fraction of Y due to unequal central tendency, to unequal variation, and to imperfect covariation. The optimal distribution of the error over the three sources is to have the covariance proportion (over which nothing can be done) equal to one and the other proportions equal to zero.

[2] G. Hildreth and J. Lu, "Demand Relationships with Autocorrelated Disturbances," Michigan State University, Agricultural Experimental Station, *Technical Bulletin 276*, Nov. 1960.

[3] W. Baumol, *Economic Dynamics* (New York: MacMillan, 1970).

[4] See, J. Ortega and W. Rheinboldt, *Iterative Solutions of Nonlinear Equations of Several Variables* (New York: Academic Press, 1970).

[5] H. Theil, *Economic Forecasts and Policy* (Amsterdam: North-Holland, 1958).

APPENDIX E

MAXIMUM LIKELIHOOD METHOD OF ESTIMATING TIME SERIES MODELS OF INTERNAL MIGRATION

The general likelihood function used to estimate the parameters of the model can be derived as follows. Let the general linear model in G jointly dependent endogenous variables and k predetermined variables be written as:[1]

(1) $By_t + \Gamma x_t = u_t$ $t = 1, 2, \ldots, n$
   where, $E(u_t) = 0$
   and $E(u_t u'_t) = \Sigma = $ a positive definite matrix

Assuming that the disturbances are normally distributed and serially uncorrelated, the likelihood function for $(u_1, u_2, \ldots, u_n)$ is then:

(2) $P(u_1, u_2, \ldots, u_n) = (2\pi)^{-nG/2}(\det \Sigma)^{-n/2} \exp(-\tfrac{1}{2} \sum_{t=1}^{n} u'_t \Sigma^{-1} u_t)$

Letting: $By_t + \Gamma x_t = [B\Gamma] \left[\begin{smallmatrix} y_t \\ x_t \end{smallmatrix} \right] = Az_t$

we can write the likelihood function for $(y_1, y_2, \ldots, y_n)$ as:

(3) $P(y_1, y_2, \ldots, y_n) = (2\pi)^{-nG/2} |\det B|^n (\det \Sigma)^{-n/2} \exp(-\tfrac{1}{2} \mathrm{tr}(\Sigma^{-1} AZ'ZA'))$

where Z is the n $\times$ (G+k) matrix of observations on all the endogenous and predetermined variables.
   If we define:

(4) $M = \dfrac{1}{n} Z'Z$

we can write the logarithm of the likelihood function as:

(5) $L(A,\Sigma) = $ constant $+ n \log |\det B| - \dfrac{n}{2} \log \det \Sigma - \dfrac{n}{2} \mathrm{tr}(\Sigma^{-1} AMA')$

The FIML estimators can be obtained by maximizing $L(A,\Sigma)$ with respect to the elements of A and using the Gauss-Gradient method of estimation.[2]

---

[1] J. Johnston, *Econometric Methods* (New York: McGraw-Hill, 1973), pp. 398–400.

[2] Y. Bard, *Nonlinear Parameter Estimation* (New York: Academic Press, 1974), Chapter 5.

The stability and steady state equilibrium of the model can be analyzed by finding solutions to the characteristic equation.[3]

The Gauss-Seidel procedure can be used for the dynamic simulation of the model.[4]

[3] W. Baumol, *Economic Dynamics.*

[4] J. Ortega and W. Rheinboldt, *Iterative Solutions of Nonlinear Equations of Several Variables.*

APPENDIX F

STATISTICAL SOURCES

The Italian South has about one-third of the population and labor force of Italy and a per capita income of 53 percent that of the Northwest, 59 percent that of the North as a whole and 65 percent of the national average. From 1958 to 1976, over one million workers (over 17 percent of the labor force of the South) emigrated to the North, of which almost 70 percent went to the Northwest (the richest, most industrialized and dynamic part of Italy).

Internal migration data in Italy is generated by a system of population registers, whereby persons changing address are legally required to report the change of address in the year he migrates. Registration is also a prerequisite for all sorts of social security benefits. People migrating abroad are also cancelled from the register of the region of departure. These data are collected and published annually (with a two-year lag) by the Central Statistical Institute (ISTAT) in *Popolazione e Movimento Anagrafico dei Comuni* and *Annuario di Statistiche Demografiche*. From 1958, they are also subdivided into workers and non-workers. The recorded 1961 net labor migration figures are inflated by about 20 to 30 percent as a result of allowing the unregistered migrants to the North of previous years to register.

Data on unemployment, percentage of the labor force employed in agriculture, and value added in industry are published annually by ISTAT in *Annuario di Statistiche del Lavoro, Supplemento Bollettino Mensile di Statistica* (N. 12, 1966) and *Annuario di Contabilita' Nazionale*; by F. Angeli in *I Conti Economici Regionali* (1974–1976), and by SVIMEZ in *Cento Anni di Statistiche Italiane, Nord et Sud* (1961). Data on industrial wages are published annually by INAIL in *Notiziario Statistico*.

BIBLIOGRAPHY

F. Angeli, ed., *I Conti Economici Regionali,* Milano, 1974-1976.

W. Baer, "Regional Inequality and Economic Growth in Brazil," *Economic Development and Cultural Change,* XII, 1964.

Banca d'Italia, *Relazioni Annuali,* Rome, 1950-1974.

Y. Bard, *Nonlinear Parameter Estimation,* Academic Press, New York, 1974.

W. Baumol, *Economic Dynamics,* MacMillan, New York, 1970.

R. Bausmann, "A Generalized Classical Method of Linear Estimation of Coefficients in a Structural Equation," *Econometrica,* XXV, 1957.

CENSIS, *Indagine sui Laureati dalle Universita' Meridionali nel 1966,* Rome, 1970.

J. Friedman, "A Generalized Theory of Polarized Development," in *Growth Centers in Regional Economic Development,* Free Press, New York, 1972.

A. Golini, *Distribuzione della Popolazione, Migrazioni Interne e Urbanizzazione in Italia,* Istituto di Demografia, Rome, 1974.

M. Greenwood, "A Simultaneous-Equations Model of Urban Growth and Migration," *Journal of the American Statistical Association,* XXX, 1975.

M. Greenwood, "An Analysis of the Determinants of Geographic Labor Mobility in the United States," *Review of Economics and Statistics,* LI, 1969.

G. Hildreth and J. Lu, "Demand Relationships with Autocorrelated Disturbances," Michigan State University, Agricultural Experimental Station, *Technical Bulletin 276,* 1960.

A. O. Hirschman, *The Strategy of Economic Development,* Yale University New Haven, 1958.

J. Harris and M. Todaro, "Migration, Unemployment and Development: A Two-Sector Analysis," *American Economic Review,* LX, 1970.

INAIL, *Notiziario Statistico,* Rome, 1951-1976.

ISTAT, *Annuario di Contabilita' Nazionale,* Rome, 1974-1977.

ISTAT, *Annuario de Statistiche del Lavoro,* Rome, 1959-1977.

ISTAT, *Annuario di Statistiche Demografiche,* Rome, 1955-1977.

ISTAT, *Popolazione e Movimento Anagrafico dei Comuni,* Rome, 1951-1977.

ISTAT, *Supplemento Bollettino Mensile de Statistica,* N. 12, Rome, 1966.

H. Johnson, *Economic Policies Toward Less Developed Countries,* Praeger, New York, 1967.

J. Johnston, *Econometric Methods,* McGraw-Hill, New York, 1973.

J. Lausén, "Regional Income Inequality and the Problem of Economic Growth in Spain," *Regional Science Association Papers and Proceedings,* 1961.

R. Muth, "Migration: Chicken or Egg," *Southern Economic Journal,* XXXVII 1971.

G. Myrdal, *An International Economy,* Harper & Row, New York, 1956.

G. Myrdal, *Rich Lands and Poor,* Harper & Row, New York, 1957.

D. Occhiuto and M. Sarcinelli, "Flussi Monetari tra Nord e Sud," *Bollettino N. 5*, Banca D'Italia, Rome, 1962.

J. Ortega and W. Rheinboldt, *Iterative Solution of Nonlinear Equations of Several Variables*, Academic Press, New York, 1970.

F. Pilloton, "Tendenze Evolutive del Mercato del Lavoro in Italia: 1951, 1971, 1991," *Studi in Onore di Pasquale Saraceno*, Giuffre', 1975.

D. Salvatore, "A Simultaneous-Equations Model of Internal Migration with Dynamic Policy Simulations and Forecasting," *Journal of Development Economics*, VII, 1980.

D. Salvatore, "A Theoretical and Empirical Evaluation and Extension of the Todaro Migration Model," forthcoming.

D. Salvatore, "An Econometric Analysis of Internal Migration in Italy," *Journal of Regional Science*, XVII, 1977.

D. Salvatore, *International Economics*, McGraw-Hill, New York, 1975.

D. Salvatore, "Interregional Capital Flows and Development," *Economia Internazionale*, XXIX, 1976.

D. Salvatore, *Microeconomic Theory*, McGraw-Hill, New York, 1974. Second Edition, 1981.

D. Salvatore, "Regional Inequality and the Market Mechanism," *Kyklos*, XXVI, 1973.

D. Salvatore, *Statistics and Econometrics*, McGraw-Hill, New York, 1981.

D. Salvatore, "Testing Various Econometric Models of Internal Migration," *Review of Regional Studies*, VII, 1977.

D. Salvatore, "The Operation of the Market Mechanism and Regional Inequality," *Kyklos*, XXV, 1972.

D. Salvatore and E. Dowling, *Development Economics*, McGraw-Hill, New York, 1977.

H. Steckler, "Forecasting with Econometric Models," *Econometrica*, XXVI, 1968.

SVIMEZ, *Cento Anni di Statistiche Italiane: Nord e Sud*, Rome, 1961.

H. Theil, *Economic Forecasts and Policy*, North-Holland, Amsterdam, 1958.

J. Williamson, "Regional Inequality and the Process of National Development," *Economic Development and Cultural Change*, XIII, 1965.

IV. EMPIRICAL ESTIMATION AND EVALUATION OF THE MODEL

1. Empirical estimation of the model

(a) Empirical results

The simultaneous-equations model of South-North net labor migration presented in Chapter III represents an overidentified system with lagged endogenous variables and first order serially correlated errors. The appropriate estimation technique used was Two-Stage Least Squares with the Hildreth-Lu scanning algorithm with grid values ranging from -1.0 to 1.0 at 0.05 intervals.[1] Briefly, the process involves: (a) the application of ordinary least squares to the reduced-form equations, (b) the applications of ordinary least squares to the transformed structural equations, the transformation consisting of the replacement of the endogenous variables by their estimated values obtained from reduced-form equations, and (c) repeating the process for each grid value of the coefficient of first order serial correlation of the errors and choosing the output with the lowest transformed error sum of squares.

The model was fit to time series data from 1958 to 1976 (see Appendix F). The results are reported in Table 2. The values in parentheis refer to the standard errors of the estimates, R^2 to the coefficient of multiple correlation, S.E.E. to the standard error of the regression, D.W. to the Durbin-Watson statistics and ϱ to the coefficient of serial correlation of the errors.

(b) Elaboration of the empirical results

From Table 2, it can be seen that the model fits the data well. *All estimated coefficients of the model have the correct sign* and operate as indicated in Chapter III. More than half of the coefficients are statistically significant at the 5 percent level and most of the other half exceed their standard errors. The R^2, measuring the proportion of the variation "explained" by the model, range from 0.7284 for the U_{St} to 0.9955 for W_{St}. No evidence of remaining serial correlation of the error terms is indicated by the Durbin-Watson statistics. ϱ is statistically significant only in equation (4), but, as indicated by the high D.W. value, its effect has been fully adjusted by the estimating techniques utilized.

---

[1] For a description of the method of estimation, see Appendix D, and Dominick Salvatore, *Statistics and Econometrics* (New York: McGraw-Hill, 1981).

31

The excellence of these empirical results in general is quite remarkable in view of the small size of the model and the complex process of internal migration and complicated pattern of interdependence within the model discussed in Chapter III.

As postulated in the model, South-North internal labor migration in Italy is strongly and directly related to the rate of unemployment in the South, the level of real wage rates in the North, the dummy, and the rate of net labor migration in the previous year. On the other hand, net South-North internal labor migration is strongly and inversely related to the rate of unemployment in the North and the level of real wages rates in the South.

As postulated in the model, the rate of unemployment in the South is inversely related to the net rate of labor migration from the South to the North and to foreign nations and to the rate of growth of real industrial value added in the South, but directly related to the natural growth of the labor force in the South and the rate of unemployment in the South in the previous period. As anticipated, the rate of unemployment in the North is inversely related to the South-North net rate of labor migration, to the growth of real industrial value added in the North and to the natural growth of the labor force in the North. On the other hand, the rate of unemployment in the North is directly related to the rate of net labor migration from the North to foreign nations and to the rate of unemployment in the North in the previous year.

As postulated in the model, the real wage rate in the South is strongly and inversely related to the rate of unemployment in the South and to the proportion of the Southern labor force in agriculture, but directly related to the real wage rate in the South in the previous period. Finally, the real wage rate in the North is strongly and inversely related to the rate of unemployment in the North but directly related to the real wage rate in the North in the previous period.

To be noted is that the results of equation (2) reported in Table 2 indicate that while both M_{SNt} and M_{SFt} have the correct negative sign, they are not statistically significant at the 5 percent level. This is due to the high degree of intercollinearity between these two variables. Conclusive proof of this is that by dropping either M_{SNt} or M_{SFt} (or by combining them into a single variable) and reestimating equation (2) in the same way, these variables retain their correct negative sign, and in every case they become statistically highly significant. However, dropping either variable biased the size of the coefficient. Furthermore, combining M_{SNt} and M_{SFt} into a single variable would have made it impossible to examine the precise relationship between U_{St} and M_{SNt} (which is crucial to the model) and to use M_{SFt} as a possible policy instrument for the development of the South (see Chapter V). The reason for M_{SNt} and M_{SFt} tending to rise and fall together is also not difficult to infer. When economic conditions in the South worsen *relative* to the North and foreign nations, these "push forces" can be expected to increase the net migration of labor from the South to both the North and foreign nations.

Table 2. Empirical Results

(1) $M_{SNt} = 0.4490 + 0.3731U_{St} - 0.4249U_{Nt} - 0.4341W_{St} + 0.3369W_{Nt} + 0.3890D + 0.4427M_{SNt-1}$
$\qquad$ (0.0995) $\quad$ (0.1519) $\quad$ (0.2098) $\quad$ (0.2067) $\quad$ (0.1662) $\quad$ (0.2081)
$\qquad R^2 = 0.9263 \quad$ S.E.E. $= 0.1350 \quad$ D.W. $= 1.9287 \quad \varrho = 0.0500$
$\qquad\qquad\qquad\qquad\qquad\qquad$ (0.2000)

(2) $U_{St} = 1.8075 - 0.5056M_{SNt} - 0.2244M_{SFt} - 0.0112Q_{St} + 0.0664L_{St} + 0.7428U_{St-1}$
$\qquad$ (0.5926) $\quad$ (0.4211) $\quad$ (0.0322) $\quad$ (0.1586) $\quad$ (0.3010)
$\qquad R^2 = 0.7284 \quad$ S.E.E. $= 0.4602 \quad$ D.W. $= 2.0183 \quad \varrho = 0.2000$
$\qquad\qquad\qquad\qquad\qquad\qquad$ (0.2449)

(3) $U_{Nt} = 2.2727 + 1.9353M^*_{SNt} + 2.5406M_{NFt} - 0.0029Q_{Nt} - 0.1482L_{Nt} + 0.4004U_{Nt-1}$
$\qquad$ (0.4120) $\quad$ (1.0567) $\quad$ (0.0180) $\quad$ (0.1136) $\quad$ (0.2029)
$\qquad R^2 = 0.7832 \quad$ S.E.E. $= 0.2478 \quad$ D.W. $= 1.9300 \quad \varrho = 0.0000$
$\qquad\qquad\qquad\qquad\qquad\qquad$ (0.0000)

(4) $W_{St} = 14.2249 - 0.4434U_{St} - 0.3245A_{St} + 0.8484W_{St-1}$
$\qquad$ (0.1665) $\quad$ (0.0761) $\quad$ (0.0844)
$\qquad R^2 = 0.9955 \quad$ S.E.E. $= 0.2611 \quad$ D.W. $= 2.2426 \quad \varrho = 0.7500$
$\qquad\qquad\qquad\qquad\qquad\qquad$ (0.1654)

(5) $W_{Nt} = 0.8613 - 0.5502U_{Nt} + 1.1391W_{Nt-1}$
$\qquad$ (0.1212) $\quad$ (0.0310)
$\qquad R^2 = 0.9942 \quad$ S.E.E. $= 0.2746 \quad$ D.W. $= 1.7572 \quad \varrho = 0.2500$
$\qquad\qquad\qquad\qquad\qquad\qquad$ (0.2421)

2. Evaluation of the model

(a) Validity simulation

More important than the statistical significance of individual parameters and a rigorous test of the validity of the model is provided by the simulation of the model over the sample period. Using the exogenous time series and the values of the endogenous variables in the previous period, the model generates historical simulated values for the endogenous variables in this period. These are then compared to the actual historical values.

The average annual simulated values of the endogenous variables generated by the model are very close to average historical values. From Table 3, it can be seen that the average annual South-North net labor migration predicted by the model is 0.9039 of the labor force of the South compared to 0.9231 historically. Thus, the model underestimates the South-North net labor migration by about 2.08 percent.[2]

Table 3   Historical and Simulated Average Annual Values, 1960–1976

	M_{SN}	U_S	U_N	W_S	W_N
Historical	0.9231	4.5706	2.7900	9.1288	10.3573
Model	0.9039	4.6127	2.8252	9.1560	10.3025
Percentage Difference	2.08	0.92	1.26	0.30	0.53

The average annual unemployment rate predicted by the model is 4.6127 percent of the labor force of the South as compared to 4.5706 percent historically, so that the model overestimates the unemployment rate of the South by 0.92 percent. The average annual unemployment rate predicted by the model is 2.8252 percent of the labor force of the North as compared to 2.79 percent historically, so that the model overestimates the unemployment rate of the North by 1.26 percent. The model predicts the average annual industrial wages in the South (in terms of 1963 prices) to be 9.1560 as compared to 9.1288 historically. The model, thus, overestimates the average real industrial wage rate of the South by 0.30 percent. Finally, the model underestimates the average annual real industrial wage of the North by 0.53 percent (10.3025 from the model as compared to 10.3573 historically).

With differences of only 2 percent or less between historical and simulated average annual values of the endogenous variables, the model performance is much better than most other larger models.[3]

[2] Note that in the simulation process two years are lost, so that Table 3 refers to the time period from 1960 (rather than 1958) to 1976.

[3] See H. Steckler, "Forecasting with Econometric Models: An Evaluation," *Econometrica*, XXXVI (1968), pp. 437–64.

(b) Short-run fluctuations

Even though the model is highly aggregative and was formulated to analyze long-run migration and other policy questions, it also captures remarkably well short-run fluctuation in the rate of South-North net labor migration and in the rate of unemployment and real wages in the South and the North. These short-run fluctuations in the historical and simulated values of M_{SN}, U_S, U_N, W_S, and W_N are shown in Figure 3.

Table 4 presents Theil's inequality coefficients (T) and their decomposition into the bias (B), variance (V) and covariance (C) proportions (see Appendix D). The T values indicate that 93 percent or more of the actual short-run change in the endogenous variables were predicted by the model. The decomposition of T into its components B, V and C is also near optimal since most of the very small divergence between historical and simulated values is due to imperfect covariation (over 80 percent in equation 4 and over 90 percent in the other equations).

Table 4 Theil's Inequality Coefficients and Their Decomposition

Endogenous Variables	T	B	V	C
Migration	0.0719	0.0186	0.0217	0.9598
Unemployment in the South	0.0439	0.0107	0.0223	0.9671
Unemployment in the North	0.0420	0.0216	0.0314	0.9470
Wages in the South	0.0134	0.0109	0.1816	0.8075
Wages in the North	0.0156	0.0262	0.0508	0.9230

3. The effect of internal migration on the South and the North

The results presented in Table 2 provide empirical evidence that South-North net labor migration reduced the average rate of unemployment and increased real wage rates over the period of the analysis both in the South and in the North. Thus, both the South and the North benefitted from internal labor migration.

The negative sign for estimated coefficients b_1 and b_2 in equation (2) in Table 2, indicates that the net labor migration from the South to the North and to foreign nations reduces the rate of unemployment in the South. The negative sign of estimated coefficient d_1 in equation (4) then indicates that this reduction in the rate of unemployment in the South, in turn, causes real wages in the South to rise. By causing the rate of unemployment in the South to fall and its real wage rate to rise, labor migration from the South thus benefits the South. The positive sign of b_4 in equation (2) also confirms the fact that in a labor-surplus economy as in the South, additions to the labor force through the natural growth of the labor force increases the rate of unemployment in the South and, through it, retards the growth of real wages in the South.

On the other hand, the negative sign of estimated coefficient c_1 and c_4 in

Figure 3   Validity Simulation: 1960–1976

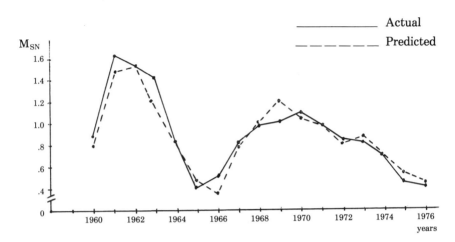

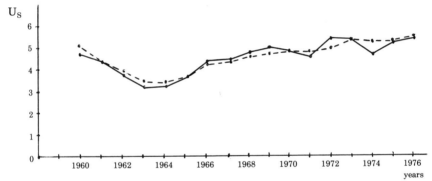

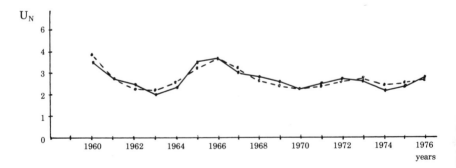

36

Figure 3   Validity Simulation: 1960–1976 — Continued

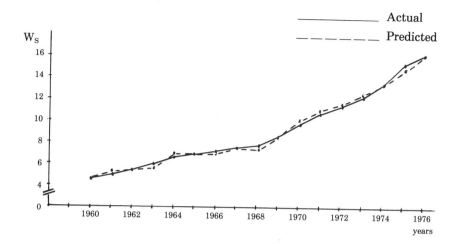

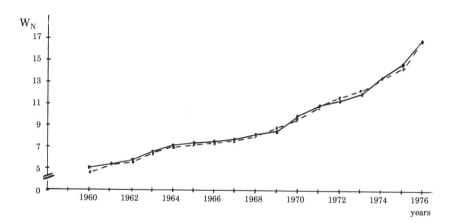

equation (3) in Table 2, indicates that in the more dynamic economy of the North, additions to the labor force through immigration from the South and through natural growth of the labor force, stimulate the economy of the North and reduce its rate of unemployment. The negative sign of estimated coefficient e_1 in equation (5) then indicates that this reduction in the rate of unemployment in the North, in turn, causes real wages in the North to rise. By causing the rate of unemployment in the North to fall and its real wage to rise, labor migration from the South thus benefits the North. The same is true for the natural increase in the labor force of the North. The positive sign of c_2 in equation (3) also confirms the point made earlier in Chapter III that if increases in the labor supply of the North (through migration from the South and through natural increases) reduces the rate of unemployment in the North, then the net *emigration* of labor from the North to other nations should increase the rate of unemployment in the North and, through it, retard the growth of real wages in the North.

The fact that net South-North labor migration benefitted the North as well as the South confirms the conclusion (based on a different and less rigorous type of analysis) reached in Chapter I and disproves Myrdal's and Hirschman's broad general assertion that internal labor migration harms the less developed region (the South).

4 The effect of migration on South-North inequalities.

In the absence of any South-North net labor migration, the average rate of unemployment would have been higher and average real wages lower both in the South and the North over the period of the analysis with respect to their actual historical values. However, South-North inequalities would be reduced only if the rate of unemployment rises less while the real wage rate falls less in the South than in the North. This important question can be answered by simulating the basic model under the assumption that M_{SN} equals to zero.[4] Table 5 presents the effect of zero net labor migration on the rate of unemployment and real wages in the South and the North and on South-North inequalities.

Table 5   Effect of No Migration (Average Annual Values)

	U_S	U_N	U_S-U_N	W_S	W_N	W_S-W_N
Basic solution	4.6127	2.8252	1.7875	9.1560	10.3025	−1.1465
No Internal Migration	5.3379	3.9703	1.3676	9.1290	9.6724	−0.5434
No Internal or Foreign Migration	5.4386	3.7870	1.6516	9.1267	9.7733	−0.6466

[4] This does not imply that internal labor migration should be stopped since that would be inconsistent with a 'free' market. The assumption of no internal labor migration is only made here in order to determine how South-North inequalities would have been affected, in the absence of any South-North net labor migration.

From Table 5, we can see that in the absence of any South-North net labor migration, U_S would be 5.3379 (instead of 4.6127 in the basic solution), U_N would be 3.9703 (instead of 2.8252 in the basic solution), so that U_S-U_N would be 1.3676 percentage points instead of 1.7875.[5] On the other hand, in the absence of any South-North net labor migration, W_S would be 9.1290 (instead of 9.1560 in the basic solution), W_N would be 9.6724 (instead of 10.3025), so that W_S-W_N would be -0.5434 (54,340 lire at 1963 prices) instead of -1.1465. Thus, while internal labor migration benefits both the South and the North, it also increases the difference in the rate of regional unemployment and real wage rates.

This seems to confirm Myrdal's and Hirschman's conclusion that internal labor migration results in increased regional differences. However, their conclusion was advanced as a *general* conclusion based on questionable analysis. As pointed out in Chapter I, the effect of net internal labor migration on the size of regional differences is basically an empirical question that depends on the circumstances under which labor migration takes place. It is easily conceivable how net South-North internal migration might reduce or leave South-North differences unchanged over a different time period than the one utilized here and for labor migration from the South to the Northwest, to the Northeast or to the Central Italy only.

Since there is likely to be a great deal of substitutability between labor migration from the South to the North and to foreign nations, it might be interesting to see how the absence of both internal and foreign migration would affect South-North inequalities. Table 5 shows that if there had been no internal *or* foreign migration, U_S-U_N would have been 1.6516 percentage points (instead of 1.7875 in the basic solution and 1.3676 in the absence of internal migration only) and W_S-W_N would have been -0.6466 (instead of -1.1465 in the basic solution and -0.5434 in the absence of internal migration only).

5. Comparison to other results

The results reported in Table 2 differ somewhat and are not directly comparable to those obtained in the other simultaneous-equations model of internal labor migration in Italy by this author.[6] The reasons for these differences are: (1) the time period covered was 1952 to 1976 in that study, while it is 1958–1976 here (the reason for the shorter time period in this study is to eliminate the need for adjustment in some of the time series); (2) the other study referred to net labor migration from the South to the Northwest, while this study examines the net labor migration from the South to the North as a

---

[5] Note that the comparison is made with the basic solution from the model rather than with the historical values in order to avoid attributing the (small) difference between the basic solution and the historical values to the absence of internal migration.

[6] Dominick Salvatore, "A Simultaneous-Equations Model of Internal Migration with Dynamic Policy Simulations and Forecasting: Italy, 1952-1976," *Journal of Development Economics*, VII (1980), pp. 231-246.

39

whole; (3) the model in my other study was in terms of *differences* in unemployment rates and real wages, while this study is more disaggregated; (4) there have been some revisions in the data base between the two studies; (5) the other model was estimated by FIML (the most powerful but seldom used estimating techniques because of its great complexity—see Appendix E) while this model was estimated by a widely accepted, sophisticated but "second best" method. Also to be pointed out is that since almost 70 percent of the net South-North labor migration went to the Northwest, the effects of internal migration were more evident and the results sharper and more clear cut in the other study, while they are more general here. As a result, these two studies can be regarded as complimentary rather than substitutes.

V. THE EFFECTIVENESS OF ECONOMIC POLICIES FOR THE DEVELOPMENT OF THE SOUTH

1. General considerations

In the model, the government has some degree of control in the long run over the growth of real value added, the percentage of the labor force employed in agriculture, the rate of labor migration to other nations, and the natural growth of the labor force. A development policy for the South could involve the attempt on the part of the government to (1) increase the growth of real value added in industry in the South, (2) reduce the percentage of the labor force employed in Southern agriculture, (3) increase the net rate of labor migration from the South to other nations, and (4) reduce the natural growth rate of the labor force in the South.

While the policy of increasing Q_S is generally acceptable, the policies of reducing A_S and L_S, and increasing M_{SF} are likely to be controversial. Furthermore, governments are, in general, more successful and willing to undertake policies to increase industrial output in the less developed region than to reduce the proportion of the labor force in agriculture and the natural growth in the labor force, and to increase the rate of net labor migration to other nations. These policies are not necessarily being advocated here. They are only examined in order to determine their effectiveness on the development of the South and on the size of South-North inequalities, *if the government was able and willing to undertake them.*

In examining the various policies, most of the attention will be on their effectiveness rather than how to carry them out. For example, we might postulate an increase in the growth of real value added in industry in the South of 25 percent over the historical growth rate, and then analyze its effect on the rate of unemployment and real wages in the South and on South-North inequalities—without a detailed and explicit consideration of how the government can best achieve this, the costs involved, and the source of the resources used. This is not to deny that some of the policies considered are very difficult to carry out or unrealistic, but it is still interesting to know what their effect would be if they had been, in fact, undertaken. In this connection, it is important to point out that all policies involve some difficulty and cost and that governments usually do not have many effective policy instruments and

41

options in their development program.

Disagreement may also arise with regard to the realism of the strength of the policies analyzed. For example, it might be thought to be impossible for the government in Italy to have been able to increase by 25 percent the growth of real value added in the South over that which actually occurred over the period of the analysis. The choice of the strength of the policies analyzed was often dictated not only by their realism but also by the necessity to have some significant measurable results. However, the effect of a possibly more moderate and realistic policy could be inferred by proportionally scaling down the results. Finally, because of some instability inherent in the model (see Appendix D), it was impossible to estimate the long-run effect of the policy measures. The results reported in this chapter refer instead to the short-run or impact effect of the policies analyzed and generally underestimate long-run results.

2. The growth of industrial output in the South

We start by examining the policy of increasing the growth of real value added in industry because governments generally have more effective control over and are more willing to affect this than other policy variables. In our model (see Chapter III), an increase in the rate of growth of real value added in industry tends to reduce the rate of unemployment in the South (equation 2) and, through it, to increase real industrial wages in the South (equation 3). These reduce the net South-North labor migration rate (equation 1) which, in turn, tends to increase the rate of unemployment in both the South and the North (equations 2 and 3) and, through them, to reduce real wages in both the South and the North (equations 4 and 5). These changes in the rate of unemployment and real wages in the South and in the North then have secondary effects on the South-North net labor migration. Simulation of the model with Q_S assumed to have been greater than historically by a specific percentage, gives the net effect on M_{SN}, U_S, U_N, W_S, W_N resulting from the complex pattern of repercussions started by the change in Q_S.

From 1958 to 1976, the average annual growth of real value added in industry was 7.17 percent in the North and 7.26 percent (but starting from a lower base) in the South. Suppose that as a result of a more decisive policy of industrialization, the growth of real value added in industry had been 25 percent higher than historically in the South (rising to an annual average of 9.08 percent) but unchanged in the North.[1] Table 6 shows that this policy (Q^*_S)

[1] From 1958 to 1976, about 6,500 billion lire at 1963 prices was spent on the industrialization of the South. This figure included the cost of providing infrastructures, incentive to private investors and directly productive investments. Thus, a rough estimate of the cost of raising the growth of real value added in industry in the South by an additional 25 percent can be put at 1,625 billion lire at 1963 prices (about 3,497 billion lire at 1976 prices). The fact that most infrastructures were already available can be expected to dampen the tendency of the incremental capital output ratio (ICOR) to rise over time.

42

Table 6. Policy Simulation Results, 1960–1976

	M_{SN}	U_S	U_N	U_S-U_N	W_S	W_N	W_S-W_N
B	0.9039	4.6127	2.8252	1.7875	9.1560	10.3025	-1.1465
Q^*_S	0.8581	4.5811	2.8410	1.7401	9.1775	10.1890	-1.0115
A^*_S	0.7840	4.6975	2.8687	1.8288	9.3187	10.1705	-0.8518
M^*_{SF}	0.8459	4.5761	2.8488	1.7273	9.1792	10.1815	-1.0023
L^*_S	0.8510	4.5792	2.8470	1.7322	9.1789	10.1824	-1.0035

Legend: B   refers to the basic solution (from Table 3) to which the other simulation runs are compared

Q^*_S the growth of real value added in industry is 25 percent higher than historically in the South but remains unchanged at actual historical levels in the North

A^*_S the proportion of the labor force employed in agriculture declines to 90 percent the actual 1976 level in the South but remains unchanged at actual historical levels in the North

M^*_{SF} the net rate of labor migration from the South to other nations is 10 percent higher than historically but is left unchanged at actual historical levels for the North

L^*_S the growth of the labor force is cut to half actual historical levels in the South but is left unchanged at actual historical levels in the North would have reduced the average South-North net rate of labor migration from 0.9039 (the basic solution) to 0.8581 or by about 47,923 workers over the period of the analysis.

Policy Q^*_S would also have *reduced* the average rate of unemployment from 4.6127 (the basic solution) to 4.5811 or by about 1,945 workers per year in the South, but *increased* the average rate of unemployment in the North from 2.8252 (the basic solution) to 2.8410 or by about 2,148 workers per year. As a result, the South-North difference in the average rate of unemployment would have fallen from 1.7875 percentage points (the basic solution) to 1.7401 percentage points.

Policy Q^*_S would have *increased* the average real industrial wage in the South from 9.1560 (the basic solution) to 9.1775 or by about 2,150 lire per year (at 1963 prices), but *reduced* the average real industrial wage in the North from 10.3025 (the basic solution) to 10.1890 or about 11,350 lire per year (at 1963 prices). As a result, the South-North difference in average real industrial wages would have fallen from -1.1465 to -1.0115 or by an average of 13,500 lire per year (at 1963 prices).

The direction of the effect of policy Q^*_S on the endogenous variables is consistent with what we expect from a theoretical analysis of the model. Specifically, the increase in Q_S reduces U_S which, in turn, increases W_S. The fall in U_S and the rise in W_S reduce M_{SN}, which then moderates the fall in U_S and, through it, the rise in W_S. The fall in M_{SN} also increases U_N which, in turn, reduces W_N. The rise in U_N and fall in W_N, together with the net fall in U_S and net rise in W_S, reduce M_{SN}.

Examining the size of these results of policy Q^*_S, we see that M_{SN} falls by a significant, although not very large amount. However, policy Q^*_S has only a very small effect on U_S and W_S.

It seems that most of the original reduction in U_S and rise in W_S from policy Q^*_S is neutralized by the repercussions from the resulting reduction in M_{SN}. On the other hand, the relatively small effect on U_N and W_N is due to the fact that the original impact of policy Q^*_S is on the South and the North only gets involved indirectly as a repercussion. It is also due to the fact that a given absolute change is proportionally much more important to the South whose economy is small relative to the economy of the North. For example, the emigration of 10,000 workers represents 0.16 percent of the labor force of the South but only 0.07 percent of the labor force of the North.

Thus, while the small effect of policy Q^*_S on the South is due to the fact that most of the original impact of Q^*_S on U_S and W_S is neutralized by the repercussions of that policy, in the North the results are relatively small because the North is involved only indirectly and because of the sheer size of the economy of the North (which includes the Northwest, Northeast and Center) in relation to the economy of the South.

3. The reduction in the proportion of the labor force in Southern agriculture

In our model, a reduction in the percentage of the labor force employed in

Southern agriculture allows a faster rise in real wage rates in the South (equation 4). This tends to reduce the net South-North labor migration rate (equation 1) which, in turn, tends to increase the rate of unemployment in both the South and the North (equations 2 and 3) and, through them, *moderate* the original *rise* in the real wage rate of the South (equation 4) but *reduce* real wage rate of the North (equation 5). These changes in the rate of unemployment and real wages in the South and in the North, then have secondary effects on the net South-North labor migration. Simulation of the model with A_S assumed to have declined faster than historically by a specific amount, gives the net effect on M_{SN}, U_S, U_N, W_S, and W_N resulting from the repercussions started from the change in A_S.

From 1958 to 1976, the percentage of the labor force employed in agriculture fell from 42.75 to 25.97 in the South and from 27.94 to 9.44 in the North. Suppose that the government succeeded in reducing the percentage of the labor force in Southern agriculture by 10 percent the actual 1976 value (a total of 159,845 workers) *without increasing the average rate of unemployment in the South* ($A*_S$). This could be done by creating more non-agricultural jobs in the South or by encouraging early retirements and more labor migration abroad from marginal and subsistence agriculture in the South. Reducing the percentage of the labor force employed in Southern agriculture by creating additional non-agricultural jobs in the South would essentially combine this policy with the policy discussed before and make it impossible to analyze the effect of each policy separately. Thus, it is here assumed that the government succeeds in carrying out policy $A*_S$ by encouraging early retirements and more labor migration abroad from marginal and subsistence agriculture in the South (otherwise most of the effect of $A*_S$ would be neutralized by the increase in U_S). Encouraging the emigration abroad of workers leaving Southern agriculture would not have any direct effect on the rate of unemployment in the South and should not be confused with policy M_{SF} (to be discussed next) which only works through its effect on U_S.[2]

Table 6 shows that policy $A*_S$ would have reduced the average South-North net rate of labor migration from 0.9039 (the basic solution) to 0.7840 or by about 125,457 workers over the period of the analysis. Policy $A*_S$ would also *increase* the average rate of unemployment from 4.6127 (the basic solution) to 4.6975 or by about 5,219 workers per year in the South, and from 2.8252 (the basic solution) to 2.8687 or by about 5,913 workers per year in the North. As a result, the South-North differences in the average rate of unemployment would have *risen* from 1.7875 percentage points (the basic solution) to 1.8288 percentage points.

Policy $A*_S$ would have *increased* average real industrial wages in the South from 9.1560 (the basic solution) to 9.3187 or by about 16,270 lire per year (at 1963 prices) in the South, but *reduced* average real industrial wages in

[2] The realism and possible difficulty of increasing the rate of net foreign migration from the South will be considered in discussing policy $M*_{SF}$.

the North from 10,3025 (the basic solution) to 10.1705 or by about 13,200 lire per year (at 1963 prices). As a result, the South-North difference in average real industrial wages would have fallen from -1.1465 to -0.8518 or by an average of 29,470 lire (at 1963 prices).

The direction of the effect of policy A^*_S on the endogenous variables is consistent with what we expect from a theoretical analysis of the model. Specifically, the more rapid reduction in A_S increases W_S which, in turn, reduces M_{SN}. This reduction in M_{SN} increases U_S and U_N, which then moderate the rise in W_S and causes W_N to fall. The rise in U_S and U_N, together with the net rise in W_S and fall in W_N, further affect M_{SN}.

Examining the size of the results of policy A^*_S, we see that M_{SN} falls by a significant amount (about 2½ times the effect of Q^*_S on M_{SN}). Policy A^*_S does not have a very large effect on U_S, W_S, and U_N and W_N. Part of the original increase of W_S is neutralized by the rise in U_S (resulting from the fall in M_{SN}). The rise in U_S and U_N are not very large because they are not affected directly by policy A^*_S but only indirectly through the fall in M_{SN}. The fall in W_N is not very large because of the small increase in U_N. Furthermore, a given change affects the South more than the North because the primary effect of the policies examined are on the South and because of the larger size of the economy of the North.

4. The increase in labor migration abroad from the South

In the model, an increase in the net rate of labor migration abroad benefits the South by reducing its rate of unemployment and raising wages. Specifically, an increase in M_{SF} tends to reduce U_S (equation 2) and, through it, to increase W_S (equation 3). These reduce M_{SN} (equation 1) which, in turn, tends to increase U_S and U_N (equations 2 and 3) and, through them, to reduce W_S and W_N. These changes in U_S and U_N, and W_S and W_N then have secondary effects on M_{SN}. Simulation of the model with M_{SF} assumed to have been greater than historically by a specific percentage, gives the net effect on M_{SN}, U_S, U_N, W_S and W_N resulting from the repercussions started by the change in M_{SF}.

From 1958 to 1976, the average net rate of labor migration abroad was 0.57 of the labor force of the South. Suppose that the government succeeded in increasing by 25 percent (i.e., to 0.71) the average net rate of labor migration from the South to other nations.[3] Table 6 shows that this policy (M^*_{SF}) would have reduced the average South-North net rate of labor migration from 0.9039

---

[3] From 1958 to 1976, a net number of 715,000 workers emigrated from the South to foreign nations. Thus, policy M^*_{SF} would have involved increasing the net outflow of migrant workers from the South to foreign nations by a total of 179,000 workers. This should not have been too difficult to achieve in view of the fact that the much larger net migration of workers from the South to foreign nations that did in fact occur took place spontaneously and without any explicit government encouragement. With the government providing information on migration possibilities, help in filling the proper forms and reducing the processing time, the M^*_{SF} policy goal could probably have been achieved easily and at very little cost. In addition to the E.E.C., Brazil, Argentina and Venezuela seemed the natural destinations since these nations were eager to absorb additional Italian labor into agriculture and construction over most of the period of the analysis.

46

(the basic solution) to 0.8459 or by about 60,688 workers over the period of analysis.

Policy M^*_{SF} would also have *reduced* U_S from 4.6127 (the basic solution) to 4.5761 or by about 2,253 workers per year in the South, but *increased* U_N from 2.8252 to 2.8488 or by about 3,207 workers per year. As a result, U_S-U_N would have fallen from 1.7875 to 1.7273 percentage points.

Policy M^*_{SF} would have *increased* W_S from 9.1560 (the basic solution) to 9.1792 or by about 2,320 lire per year (at 1963 prices), but *reduced* W_N from 10.3025 to 10.1815 or by about 12,100 lire per year (at 1963 prices). As a result, W_S-W_N would have fallen from -1.1465 to -1.0023 or by an average of 14,420 lire per year (at 1963 prices).

The direction of the effect of policy M^*_{SF} on the endogenous variables is consistent with what we expect from a theoretical analysis of the model. Specifically, the increase in M_{SF} reduces U_S which, in turn, increases W_S. The fall in U_S and the rise in W_S reduce M_{SN}, which then moderates the fall in U_S and, through it, the rise in W_S. The fall in M_{SN} also increases U_N which, in turn, reduces W_N. The rise in U_N and fall in W_N, together with the net fall in U_S and net rise in W_S, reduce M_{SN}.

Policy M^*_{SF} results in a significant, although not very large, fall in M_{SN}, but has only a small effect on U_S and W_S, and U_N and W_N. It seems that most of the original reduction in U_S and rise in W_S from policy M^*_{SF} is neutralized by the repercussions from the resulting reduction in M_{SN}. On the other hand, the relatively small effect on U_N and W_N is due to the fact that the original impact of policy M^*_{SF} is on the South and the North only gets involved indirectly as a repercussion. It is also due to the fact that the economy of the North is much larger than the economy of the South.

5. The reduction in the natural growth of the labor force in the South

The policy of reducing the natural growth of the labor force in the South is the most controversial of the policies discussed and the most difficult to carry out. Except in some very poor countries such as India and China, governments have been reluctant to have a strong explicit and direct population policy. Such a policy implies a degree of regimentation and interference with personal freedom that is generally unacceptable in today's more democratic societies. In addition, there is often strong religious opposition to the policy. Because of individual and religious opposition, tradition and lack of education and information, this policy was usually not very successful whenever tried. More realistic would be to favor early retirements and the raising of the legal age for entering the labor force.

There is strong empirical evidence indicating that the natural growth of the population (and labor force) is strongly affected only as the natural result of economic and social development. Furthermore, with the period of the analysis of only 19 years, compared with 14 as the legal age for entering the labor force in Italy, not much could have been achieved even if this policy had been desired and tried. As a result, the reduction in the natural growth of the population and labor force in the South will not be regarded as the policy variable on par with the others. We will only analyze how the economy of the South and South-North differences would have been affected *if* the natural growth rate of the South had been smaller than historically by a given amount—without either advocating or making this reduction the result of any specific population policy.

In the model, a reduction in the natural growth rate of the labor force of the South would have benefitted the South by reducing its rate of unemployment and raising wages. Another important benefit would have been the avoidance of the heavy burden of raising, educating and training more workers than could find fruitful employment in the South.

A reduction in L_S tends to reduce U_S (equation 2) and, through it, to increase W_S (equation 3). The other effects and repercussions are the same as for policies $Q*_S$ and $M*_{SF}$.

From 1958 to 1976, the labor force of the South *in the absence of any migration* grew at an average of 0.76 percent (about 46,778) per year. This reflected new entrants into the labor force, departures at retirement age and an 18 percent decline in the participation rate (from 38.38 in 1958 to 31.59 in 1976). Suppose that the government succeeded in cutting to one-half (i.e., to 0.38 percent) the average yearly growth of the labor force in the South over the period of the analysis.[4] Table 6 shows that this policy $(L*_S)$ would have reduced the average South-North net rate of labor migration from 0.9039 to 0.8510 or by about 55,352 workers over the period of the analysis.

Policy $L*_S$ would also have reduced U_S from 4.6127 to 4.5792 or by about 2,062 workers per year in the South, and increased U_N from 2.8252 to 2.8470 or by about 2,963 workers per year. As a result, U_S-U_N would have fallen from 1.7875 to 1.7322 percentage points.

Policy $L*_S$ would have increased W_S from 9.1560 to 9.1789 or by about 2,290 lire per year (at 1963 prices), and reduced W_N from 10.3025 to 10.1824 or by about 12,010 lire per year (at 1963 prices). As a result, W_S-W_N would have fallen from -1.1465 to -1.0035 or by about 14,300 lire per year (at 1963 prices).

The direction of the effect of policy $L*_S$ on the endogenous variables is consistent with what we would expect from a theoretical analysis of the model, and are the same as for policies $M*_{SF}$ and $Q*_S$. The size of the results of policy $L*_S$ are also similar to those of policies $M*_{SF}$ and $Q*_S$, and for the same reasons.

6. Policy conclusions

Since the policies presented in this chapter are directed at the development of

---

[4] Part of this reduction could have been achieved by encouraging early retirements in marginal occupations in the South.

the South, their original effect is on the South, with the North affected only indirectly from the repercussions of the change in M_{SN}. Policies Q^*_S, M^*_{SF} and L^*_S originally affect only U_S (equation 2), and W_S, M_{SN}, U_N and W_N only secondarily as repercussions. Policy A^*_S originally affects only W_S (equation 4), and M_{SN}, U_S, U_N and W_N only secondarily as repercussions.

Policy A^*_S has the most significant effect on W_S, M_{SN}, U_S and U_N, while Q^*_S has the smallest effect. Policy Q^*_S is the most realistic, while L^*_S is the least possible and realistic to carry out. Except for their effect on M_{SN}, policies Q^*_S, A^*_S, M^*_{SF} and L^*_S do not seem to have a significant effect on U_S, U_N, W_S and W_N. The effects of these policies in the South are not very large because the secondary effects or repercussions of the various policies always neutralize part of the original effect. Effects in the North are not very large because the North is only indirectly involved from the secondary or tertiary repercussions of the policies discussed. The effectiveness of these policies is also small because the length of the time period of the analysis over which these policies operate is relatively short and because only the short-run or impact effect of these policies could be measured.

All policies reduce W_S-W_N, and all but A^*_S also reduce U_S-U_N. The reductions in U_S-U_N are not very large and are generally smaller than the changes in W_S-W_N.

If any general policy conclusions can be reached from this chapter, it is that the government does not seem to have many very effective general policy instruments at the macro level to use for the development of the South. At least this seems the case from analyzing and applying the model presented in Chapter III.

Finally, if the future can be predicted from the past, outmigration of labor from the South to the North is likely to continue for some years to come. The South-North gap is likely to rise without a larger development effort for the South and, in any event, it is likely to persist for many more years. Thus, the goal of the Italian Government to eliminate North-South differences are as elusive today as it was a generation ago. This, however, does not mean that the large development effort for the South has been a failure. The difficulties inherent in transforming a traditional and backward economy into one that is economically and socially advanced have generally proven to be much more stubborn and difficult than it was believed in the immediate post war years. The development of a generally acceptable and effective development theory has itself proven to be very elusive. It is safe to conclude that in the absence of the large development effort under the direction of the CASSA per il Mezzogiorno, the North-South gap would have been much larger than it is. In this sense, the development effort for the South has been very successful.